What You Need to Know About Cannabis

by the same authors

Getting Wise to Drugs
A Resource for Teaching Children about Drugs, Dangerous Substances and Other Risky Situations
David Emmett and Graeme Nice
ISBN: 978 1 84310 507 7

Understanding Drug Issues
A Photocopiable Resource Workbook
2nd edition
David Emmett and Graeme Nice
ISBN: 978 1 84310 350 9

Understanding Street Drugs
A Handbook of Substance Misuse for Parents, Teachers and Other Professionals
2nd edition
David Emmett and Graeme Nice
ISBN: 978 1 84310 351 6

What You Need to Know About Cannabis

Understanding the Facts

David Emmett and Graeme Nice

Jessica Kingsley Publishers
London and Philadelphia

First published in 2009
by Jessica Kingsley Publishers
116 Pentonville Road
London N1 9JB, UK
and
400 Market Street, Suite 400
Philadelphia, PA 19106, USA

www.jkp.com

Library of Congress Cataloging in Publication Data
Emmett, David.
  What you need to know about cannabis : understanding the facts / David Emmett and Graeme Nice.
     p. cm.
  Includes bibliographical references and index.
  ISBN 978-1-84310-697-5 (pb : alk. paper) 1. Cannabis. I. Nice, Graeme. II. Title.
  HV5822.C3E46 2009
  362.29'5--dc22
                              2008022624

British Library Cataloguing in Publication Data
A CIP catalogue record for this book is available from the British Library

ISBN 978 1 84310 697 5

Printed and bound in the United States by
Thomson-Shore, 7300 Joy Road, Dexter, Michigan, United States, 48130

Contents

Introduction

Working as substance misuse counsellors and educators over many years, we have gathered a wealth of experience in dealing directly with cannabis users, and others indirectly affected by its use. It has become clear to us that there is a high degree of confusion and ignorance surrounding this particular drug, perhaps more so than with some other illegal substances. There are those who wish to promote cannabis as a harmless, even beneficial substance, whilst others take the opposite view and wish the public to view cannabis as 'devil weed', responsible for many of society's problems.

In our view neither of these two positions is supported by the evidence currently available. It is our intention in writing this book to examine and present a balanced account of the information currently available, covering as many aspects as possible, in order to provide you with what you need to know to form your own opinions about this controversial drug.

We have met many cannabis users who have claimed to use the drug with no ill effects; however, in recent years much clinical research, from countries around the entire globe, has been published which draws attention to the significant links between cannabis use and a number of serious long-term mental health problems. Other research has identified a clear physical addiction and accompanying withdrawal syndrome of clinically important symptoms, especially in heavy users. Similarly, it has been demonstrated that a small percentage of users are more genetically susceptible to problems with the drug.

With so much new information being made available, some of it apparently contradictory, we believe that a clear need exists to set out, in as easily understandable and accessible way as possible, many of the diverse issues that have surfaced, drawing on a wide range of sources.

You need to be aware that research in this field is ongoing, and further information may become available that requires a modification of that informed view.

Therefore, this book should not be considered as the 'last word' on the subject of cannabis, as knowledge is constantly increasing and evolving. Still, we hope that within these pages we have covered sufficient ground to provide you with 'what you need to know', and to help you arrive at your own position on this important subject.

Chapter One

Cannabis – the Plant and the Drug

Figure 1.1: Cannabis sativa *growing in the open*

Cannabis is an annual flowering plant of the botanical order *Rosales* which today occurs wild across large parts of the world, thriving in a wide range of soil types in countries from the temperate regions to those in the tropics. Other well-known members of the *Rosales* order include hops and nettles. The cannabis plant seems to have originated in countries lying to the east and south-east of the Caspian Sea in Western Asia; indeed, the world's largest areas of wild unculti-vated cannabis are to be found in the countries of Kazakhstan and Kyrgyzstan. However, almost certainly as a result of human involvement with the plant, it is now found growing either wild or under cultivation across the entire globe.

Three main varieties belong to the genus cannabis:[1] *Cannabis sativa*, the fastest-growing variety, reaching two to four metres in height in a single season; *Cannabis indica* and *Cannabis ruderalis*, both slower growing and generally not reaching more than two metres in height.

In an effort to increase yield and potency, growers across the world have interbred these three varieties to produce hybrid types. Through a process of cloning, enormous quantities of true breeding seeds from these hybrids are now available. This topic will be covered in more detail later, in the section dealing particularly with indoor cultivation.

All three natural varieties produce within them a number of complex chemicals called cannabinoids. The most psychoactive of these, and thus the most important in recreational drug terms, is $\Delta 9$ Tetrahydrocannabinol,[2] known commonly as THC. Of the three varieties, *Cannabis sativa* produces THC in the highest concentrations and has historically been the preferred variety of the plant. In sexual terms cannabis plants are known as *Dioecious* – that is, there are two distinct forms, a male and a much larger female. Both genders produce THC but the amount produced by the female is significantly higher than that produced by the male. In order to make the THC available to the user, the plant is prepared for use in three major ways, resulting in herbal cannabis, cannabis resin and cannabis oil.:

Herbal cannabis

Some slang names for herbal cannabis

Marijuana, grass, weed, herb, blow, puff, bush, wacky baccy, dope, tips, buds, sinsy, sinse, sinsemilia, skunk, super-skunk, draw, sativa, ganja, dagga, hemp, homegrown, tea, hay, kief.

Herbal cannabis is at its simplest the dried and chopped leaves and flowers of the cannabis plant, usually compressed into bales of varying sizes. The finest quality and most potent herbal cannabis is produced by drying and chopping the flowers, known as the buds, of the female cannabis plant as it approaches sexual maturity. This type of herbal cannabis known on the streets as *bud* and sometimes as *sinsemilia*, *sinse* or *sinsy* contains the highest levels of THC in herbal form and attracts the highest prices. Traditionally almost all of this bud-type herbal cannabis was produced using female flowers from the *Cannabis sativa* plant.

Figure 1.2: Herbal and resin cannabis

However, in recent times, it has become increasingly common for the female flowers of hybrid varieties such as those known as *skunk* or *super-skunk* to be used in this process. Less potent, and therefore cheaper, herbal cannabis is produced by mixing quantities of dried flower and dried leaves in differing ratios.

Generally the higher levels of THC are to be found in leaves of the female plant and in particular those growing near to the flowering top of the plant. Thus, the best of these cheaper types consist of a high ratio of flowers together with upper female leaves. The slang name *tip* or *tips* is sometimes used to describe such herbal cannabis. However, drug producers are often more interested in the quantity of saleable drug that they can produce rather than its quality, and so much of the herbal cannabis reaching the retail customer is of generally poor quality, and thus of low potency. It can consist of a mixture of chopped leaves of all sizes from both the female and male plant, stems, small quantities of flower bud and some seeds.

Another issue that affects quality is that of adulteration. Much of the herbal cannabis on the world's streets has been adulterated with other substances, some of which are in themselves harmless and some of which may represent potential health risks to the user. Most adulterants have been added to bulk out and thus increase the weight of the product. This will often have been done within the source country of the drug but is also often carried out by small suppliers at street level to increase their sales profits. Some adulterants are added to disguise the poor quality of the product or to fool the customer into believing it to be a higher quality or more potent variety, for example by adding colouring agents and oils in imitation of herbal types containing higher quantities of resin.

Attention has been drawn by a number of agencies in recent times to the adulteration of herbal cannabis with minute beads of glass. Claims have been made that high-quality female flowering cannabis heads often have a slight 'sparkle' and that adding glass beads to cheaper mixes is done with the intention of giving the resultant product a similar 'sparkle'. The topic of cannabis contaminated with glass beads and the health implications of other adulterants will be discussed in more detail in Chapter 2.

Most samples of herbal cannabis that we have seen are a greenish brown or greyish green in colour, although on rare occasions samples are seen that are purple, pale green or golden. Parents, teachers and others with responsibility for young people often think they have discovered herbal cannabis in the possession of one of their charges when, in fact, what they have found is loose tobacco. Herbal cannabis can be mistaken by those without experience for various forms of tobacco due to its similar appearance. However, close examination of the material should eliminate that mistake. Most samples of tobacco have been produced by chopping dried plugs of tobacco leaves that have been formed from several leaves from different tobacco varieties layered together and cured. This layering can be seen in the form of strata of differing colours in the small shreds of tobacco. Cannabis has no such layering. Round seeds, approximately 5 mm in diameter, are often found in herbal cannabis whereas tobacco contains no such seeds. Tobacco often has a strong, aromatic smell, whereas most herbal cannabis simply smells a little musty. In some samples of the modern skunk and super-skunk varieties, this musty smell can be strong enough to be unpleasant, hence the names.

Cannabis resin

Some slang names for cannabis resin

Pot, hash, hashish, shit, charas, black, gold, soap, red leb, China black, double zero, flat press, red seal, rocky, solid, black ganga, Moroccan, block, rez, blonde.

Cannabis resin is produced by collecting, drying and pressing the resinous exudate of the cannabis plant, particularly the female plant. These produce small hairs called 'trichomes' all over their leaves and flower buds. As the plants approach sexual maturity they begin to exude tiny sticky beads of a colourless resinous liquid which contains a high percentage of THC. The trichomes that are found all over the flower or bud of the female plant exude the largest amounts of this THC-laden liquid. The liquid acts to absorb ultraviolet B (UV-B) light and therefore serves as a natural sunscreen for the plant. As a consequence, when in bright sunshine, the plant produces more liquid at the end of each of its trichomes, and the flower then often has a sparkly appearance. It is this liquid exudate that forms the basis of all cannabis resin.

We have seen resin in a wide variety of colours, consistencies and forms. The variations in colour and consistency are mostly a result of differences in climate and soil conditions between the various countries where the plant was grown, the methods used to collect the exudate, and the expertise and thoroughness of the producer.

Resin colour can vary from the deepest black, through slate grey and every shade of brown that you can imagine, to a pale honey or straw colour. Some black forms are hard, shiny and brittle, and can be snapped easily. Dark brown, fine-grain resins tend to be very hard and dense and very difficult to break up. The user often has to heat the resin block with a flame before being able to crumble it for use, a process often called 'roasting' or 'toasting'. Many of the paler coloured resins are soft and dry and crumble easily in the fingers. Reports reach us every so often of resin being sold in the form of an oily, putty type of material. This product appears to consist of one of the more normal varieties of resin that has had oil added to it. This may actually be cannabis oil, or in many cases any one of a number of other unknown oils. The purpose of adding oil would seem to be in order to make the resin look of better quality.

Whether cannabis resin is being prepared on a large scale under traditional conditions in countries with a long history of cannabis production, on a smaller scale in modern indoor growing facilities, or under 'kitchen table' conditions, the three basic methods remain the same.

Threshing and sieving

'Threshing and sieving' is a traditional method of producing cannabis resin and is the most widely used method for commercial resin production. When sufficient numbers of people are involved in the process, it can be very efficient and is often used to produce enormous quantities. It is the favoured method of resin production in traditional growing countries such as Lebanon, Morocco,

Afghanistan, India and Jamaica. The process is designed to separate and collect the THC-laden trichomes.

The plants are first harvested and laid out to dry. It is perhaps more common today for security reasons for this drying to take place entirely out of sight inside a barn or storeroom. The grower will not wish to disturb the plant during this process any more than is necessary so as to avoid dislodging the drying trichomes. Once the crop is dry, the plants are prepared for threshing and sieving. Some producers will remove the dried female flowers for separate processing in order to obtain the highest quality resin containing the highest percentage of THC. Other producers will remove all of the larger stems and leaves to leave only flowers and thin stems with small leaves. This will lead to the production of resin of medium quality. Producers seeking to produce large quantities of low-quality resin will use the whole plant including male and female types, large and small leaves, stems of all sizes and some flowers.

Following drying, the plant is broken up and placed in the first of a series of sieves. The plant material is then agitated or threshed vigorously back and forth in the sieve, so that the dried trichomes are dislodged and pass through the sieve along with small particles of plant material. The resulting mixture is then passed through another sieve with a smaller mesh. This separates out further particles of plant material and allows through only very small particles. This process is continued through a series of sieves each finer than the one before. Only the minute particles of dried resinous sap, with the high THC level found on the heads of the trichomes, can pass through the final sieve.

The material that fails to pass through each sieve, with the possible exception of the remains of stem, old leaves and seeds that remain from the first sieving, is also collected for sale. It will contain varying percentages of THC. What remains in sieves early in the process will contain less THC than that from later finer sieves. The material resulting from this process is then pressed into blocks of different shapes and sizes. Producers will often emboss the pressed blocks with a name or character to identify it as their product.

The traditional processes of threshing and sieving have been adopted by today's growers, both small and large scale. A number of websites exist that offer sieves and other equipment for use in this process, including a number of motorized threshers and sieves, thus removing the human labour completely.

Rubbing

Sometimes referred to as 'manual separation', the process of rubbing to collect cannabis resin is uncomplicated. It consists of rubbing the cannabis plant to break up the THC-laden trichomes and collecting the resin that is released. At its simplest, this consists of rubbing the stems, leaves and flowers of the cannabis plant with the hands, which become coated in fresh resin. This is then removed by rubbing the hands together until a small ball of resin is produced. This is a process that can be repeated on the same plant a number of times during its life cycle. The most productive time occurs as the plant reaches sexual maturity, in other words as it flowers, and for a short time afterwards. Trichomes that are removed by rubbing at this stage will be replaced with fresh growth that can be harvested in its turn.

Another traditional method of manual separation is to use a tool to scrape the trichomes from the plant. These can be made from glass, ceramics or metal, and the resin collected on them is then peeled off and rolled into a ball. This is not as effective as hand rubbing as it is difficult with a tool to reach all parts of the plant. However, it is a lot cleaner!

We have heard of a lot of other unusual and eccentric methods used. One grower related to us how he gently beat his plants with a bamboo cane and then peeled the resin off. Another story that we have heard is of growers dressing in leather jeans and jacket and running back and forth amongst plants in an outdoor plantation, so that their clothes become encrusted with resin. Whatever the exact method used, the intention is to break off the trichomes to release the resin.

Water extraction

The last of the three methods described in this volume relies on the high specific gravity of resin, as compared with the rest of the cannabis plant. It is a very simple method that is popular with small-scale growers. The basic method is to dry the cannabis plant until it can be pulverized easily. The dry plant is then rubbed through a sieve into a container of water. The heavy resin will fall to the bottom whilst the lighter plant material floats on top. The resin is recovered by decanting off the water, and then dried before pressing. A number of websites offer equipment for use in this process.

Cannabis oil

Some slang names for cannabis oil

Oil, hash oil, honey, diesel, red oil, Indian oil, weed oil.

The last of the three traditional forms of cannabis is by far the rarest. This can be calculated from the global seizure figures, discussed later.

Cannabis oil is produced by mixing either cannabis resin or plant material itself with a solvent such as grain alcohol, denatured alcohol, naptha, acetone, etc. The solvent will disolve the resin, whilst the plant material is left untouched and removed. The solvent is then evaporated off leaving behind a viscous oil that contains a very high level of THC. The oil will vary in colour from a pale honey colour to dark green or dark brown to black, and in viscosity from thin and runny to a highly viscous treacle-like consistency. Cannabis oil can have a very powerful smell similar to rotting vegetation.

Special note

It is worth making the point that despite the differences between the various forms of cannabis, the active ingredient remains simply Δ9 Tetrahydrocannabinol.

Methods of use

Globally, the most common method of using cannabis is to smoke it. Smoking can be a highly effective way of getting any drug into the body. THC passes readily through the outer membrane of the pulmonary capillaries in the lungs and then into the bloodstream and thus to the central nervous system.

Cannabis can be smoked in a number of different ways, but, whatever way is chosen, there are several practical problems for the user to overcome. First, herbal cannabis is often dry and short stranded, unlike tobacco which is moist and long stranded. It does not cling together in the way tobacco does and is therefore not an easy substance to make into cigarettes. Second, it burns at a higher temperature than tobacco, and if the user does not take some measures to deal with that degree of extra heat then it can burn the lips, tongue and throat. Third, the average street sample of cannabis contains a higher amount of tar than commercially available tobacco cigarettes.[3]

Hand-rolled joints

By far the commonest method of smoking cannabis is to roll it in a hand-rolled cigarette, most commonly called a *joint* or a *spliff.* Smokers who have sufficient herbal cannabis will usually construct, build or 'skin up' their joint without adding any tobacco at all. In order to smoke cannabis resin in a joint, it is necessary to crumble it and then mix it with either herbal cannabis or, much more commonly, tobacco.

The smoker will often use one of the commercially produced 'king-sized' cigarette rolling papers to construct their joint. Millions of packets of king-sized cigarette papers are sold every year in a bewildering array of colours including black. One brand is advertised as being transparent, others patterned with designs such as fruits, candies or bank notes. The packets the papers are sold in are often decorated with all sorts of cannabis imagery. Alongside a number of well-known proprietary brands, a quick search of the Internet will reveal thousand of websites ready to sell such papers. It is even possible to purchase ready rolled paper tubes that simply require filling, and small highly coloured plastic tubes to keep the joint safe in one's pocket.

When constructing the joint, the cannabis or cannabis/tobacco mixture is placed on the paper, and, before sealing, a small cylinder called a *roach* or *tip* is added at the end to be placed in the mouth. This cylinder is commonly made from a small piece of cardboard, usually torn from the cigarette paper packet cover, that is rolled up tight and then allowed to relax. It forms into a rough spiral which serves two purposes. First, it acts as a mesh to keep the smoking mixture inside the cigarette and stop it coming out into the mouth; second, it positions the burning end of the cigarette a little further away from the smoker's mouth thus alleviating a little of the heat problem. As with the cigarette papers, there are a large number of websites selling small packs of ready cut card to use as roaches. In recent years we have come across a substantial number of what are called *roach cards*. These are usually colourful advertisements for a commercial product or an upcoming musical event, printed on a postcard-sized piece of thin card that has been perforated into perfect roach-sized oblongs. The receiver of the card can read the advertisement and then break the card up into its oblongs and use them in the construction of their joints.

There is a fashion amongst cannabis smokers for making joints in all sorts of extravagant shapes and sizes. Super-size joints are made using five or even seven papers (*skins*); some are as large as a corona cigar and are used as 'party joints', being intended for several people to share. The 1986 cult British film *Withnail and I* featured such a super-size joint that was referred to by the person rolling it as a 'Camberwell Carrot'. Curious shapes are sometimes constructed often with more than one burning end. There are a number of freely available publications and websites which give instructions to users in making joints of all sorts. A variation on the joint is called a *blunt*, created by carefully hollowing out a cigar and filling it with cannabis. Ready-prepared hollow cigars are available from a number of websites for this purpose.

Water pipes

The traditional way of smoking cannabis using a hookah or hubble bubble pipe is still very popular. Expensive hand crafted and decorative water pipes made from the finest materials are to be found for sale in most European countries, and on a vast number of Internet websites. Such sites also sell a huge array of well-made modern versions of the traditional water pipe. These are constructed from everything from ceramics, glass, acrylic, wood and even stainless steel and, whilst all operating on the same principle, can be very ingenious in their construction. Many sites sell what are called 'party pipes' which are fitted with a number of mouthpieces allowing a group of people to share the same pipe. Water pipes made from much poorer quality materials are sold legally, and at very low cost, on market stalls and in certain shops, and many are brought back home from countries in North Africa and the Middle East by tourists as innocent holiday souvenirs.

The operating principle is basically the same for all these water pipes: the smoke from the burning cannabis passes through a container of water before reaching the smoker. The water acts to cool the smoke and remove some of the tars from it. An Internet search using the search phrase 'cannabis pipes' will reveal to the reader the vast selection available. However, for many people it is

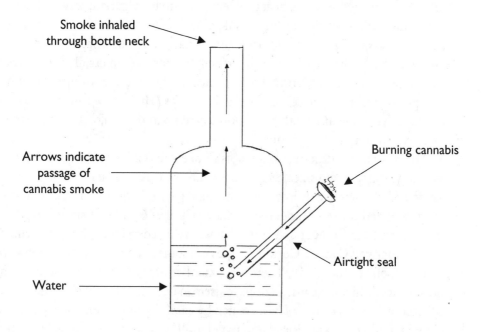

Figure 1.3: Homemade bhong

still common for a crude version called a *bhong* or *bong* to be constructed using a wide assortment of different household objects that can be made watertight.

At its simplest, such a pipe will be constructed from a plastic bottle of around one litre in size. A hole is pierced in the side of the bottle about halfway up and a tube inserted at a downwards angle until its end reaches close to the bottom. A waterproof seal is then made between the side of the bottle and the tube with chewing gum or some other sealant material. The tube may be made from plastic, glass, wood, rubber or metal. At the upper end of the tube a smoking bowl will be constructed using punctured tin foil and fixed to the tube end. We have seen bottle tops used as bowls and more robust smoking bowls made from mechanic's sockets which have had a hole drilled through the base of them. The bottle is partially filled with water until the lower end of the tube is covered and the bhong is ready for use. The smoking bowl is filled with a cannabis mixture and is lit while the smoker inhales through the neck of the bottle. Inhaling creates a depression over the water and smoke is drawn from the burning cannabis down the tube to bubble up through the water to the smoker's mouth.

This is the most basic design of the bhong, but there are many variations on this theme. Over the years we have seen bhongs made from all sorts of containers, from brandy bottles, chemical retorts, ball valve floats, buckets, and on one occasion from a dustbin in which the smoking bowl was an old saucepan, the plumbing was made from pieces of garden hose, and the bhong equipped with six mouthpieces. We have also seen multi-chamber bhongs in which the smoke is drawn through more than one water chamber before reaching the smoker. Clearly the more chambers one uses, the cooler the smoke reaching the user will be. However, the ability of the user to draw the smoke through limits the number of chambers that can be used.

A particular technique of smoking cannabis using water is often called *bucketing*, using a gravity water bhong. The bottom is cut out of a large plastic bottle. A bucket-sized container is filled with water and the upright bottle pushed down into it. This fills the body of the bottle with water. A smoking bowl is fashioned and fitted to the neck of the bottle and filled with the cannabis mixture. The mixture is lit and the bottle raised until its base is still just immersed in the water. This action draws the cannabis smoke down into the bottle. The smoking bowl is then removed and the smoker places their mouth over the neck of the bottle. The smoker then pushes the bottle back down into the water, thus forcing the smoke out of the bottle into their mouth.

A variety of this is called a *reverse gravity pipe*. In this device the drinks bottle has a hole made in the bottom of it which is sealed with a small stopper. The bottle is filled with water and the smoking bowl fitted to its neck. The cannabis is lit and the stopper removed, and, as the water escapes from the bottle, smoke is

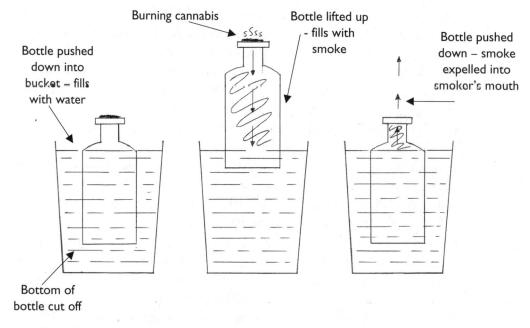

Burning cannabis

Bottle lifted up
- fills with
smoke

Bottle pushed
down – smoke
expelled into
smoker's mouth

Bottle pushed
down into
bucket – fills
with water

Bottom of
bottle cut off

Figure 1.4: Gravity pipe

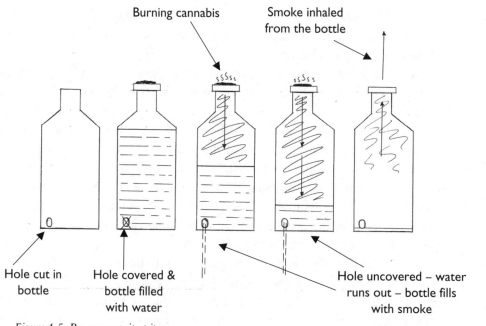

Burning cannabis

Smoke inhaled
from the bottle

Hole cut in
bottle

Hole covered &
bottle filled
with water

Hole uncovered – water
runs out – bottle fills
with smoke

Figure 1.5: Reverse gravity pipe

drawn down into it. Once the bottle is filled, the smoking bowl is removed and the user inhales from the bottleneck.

Another variation on this is a pipe known as a *lung*, manufactured from a small plastic drinks bottle. The bottom is cut off and a plastic bag is fixed over the base with sticky tape and pushed or 'sucked' up inside the bottle. A smoking bowl is fitted to the neck of the bottle. Cannabis is added to the bowl and lit. The plastic bag is then pulled down slowly to draw the smoke into the bottle and bag. The smoking bowl is then removed and the user then slowly pushes the plastic bag back inside the bottle to drive the smoke out of the bottle into the mouth. The lung may be passed round a group until all the smoke has been used up and the process repeated.

Cannabis
burning bowl

Plastic bag 'lung'
pushed or
sucked up into
bottle

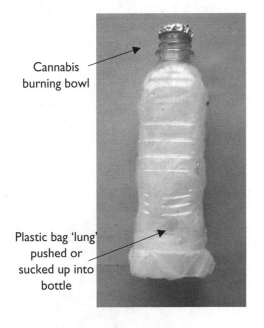

'Lung' pulled
down – drawing
smoke into bottle

Figure 1.6: Homemade lung

We have seen at least one commercially available pipe that uses this design. It takes the form of a colourful plastic ball with a mouthpiece and smoking bowl fitted. The plastic bag used in the homemade version has been replaced with a plastic concertina tube. The smoker lights the mixture and allows the concertina tube to extend downwards under its own weight, filling with smoke. The pipe is then used in the same way as the homemade version.

Chillum pipes

Many smokers use a form of pipe called a *chillum* to smoke their cannabis. Chillum pipes are usually purchased ready made but can be homemade. The design of a traditional chillum pipe involves a hole drilled straight through the stem of the pipe from the mouthpiece and passing under the smoking bowl to open at the front of the pipe. The smoking bowl has an opening at its base which leads into this drilling. The smoker places a finger over the front opening of the drilling and is thus able to close or open this hole to regulate air drawn into the smoke coming from the bowl, to both cool and dilute it. This type of chillum pipe is often made from tropical hard woods, soapstone or ceramics. Many modern cannabis pipes sold as chillums do not feature this opening in the front, and are made from a variety of very colourful materials including glass and metal.

High-tech pipes

A more recent addition to the range of cannabis smoking implements is a variety of high-tech pipes. These are often made from metal and take a number of forms, from something the size of a rather thick credit card to a finger-sized cylinder. All feature extended internal smoke passages leading from the burning bowl to

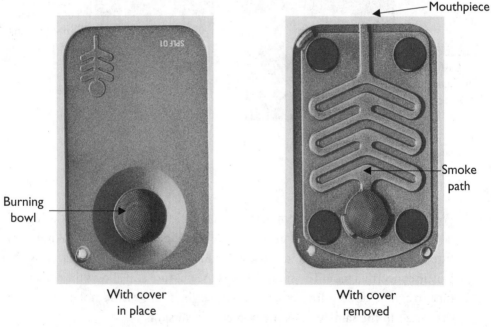

Figure 1.7: High-tech chillum – known as a 'palm pipe'

the mouthpiece. This extended pipework is to allow for the cooling of the hot cannabis smoke. Many of these modern designs would not be recognized by any uninitiated person as being connected to any form of drug use. An example of one such pipe we have seen looked like a flat sheet of thin metal 50mm x 80mm, but featured an internal smoke path 320mm long. Again an Internet search for 'cannabis pipes' will educate the reader in what to look out for.

Vaporizers

Some cannabis users prefer to inhale the THC and other cannabinoids without also inhaling the products of combustion that result from burning the drug. In recent years a large range of different devices called vaporizers has appeared on the market to service this need. Some of these are high specification pieces of equipment powered by electricity. The designs vary in detail but in essence all work in similar ways. The cannabis is placed on a hot plate enclosed in a glass or plastic dome. The hot plate is heated to around 180°C to 200°C, which is sufficient to begin the vaporization of the THC and other cannabinoids within the cannabis mixture, whilst remaining below the temperature at which cannabis ignites. The vapour collects within the dome and is drawn by the user along a tube to the mouthpiece.

Other much simpler versions of this are similar in appearance to more ordinary smoking pipes. They consist of a glass bubble with a ventilated opening and a mouthpiece. The pipe is opened and the cannabis mixture inserted into the bubble. This is then heated from underneath with a naked flame until the

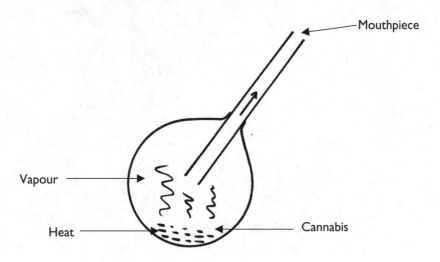

Figure 1.8: Simple glass vaporizer

mixture begins to visibly emit vapour. The vapour is then drawn to the mouth-piece by the user.

Toke cans

Another form of pipe used for the smoking of cannabis is the *toke* or *toke can*. These remain popular with many young people as they take only a few seconds to prepare. The user takes an empty drinks can and uses the thumb to make a depression in the side of the can near to the base. This depression is made in line with the ring pull opening and on the same side of the can. A few holes are punctured in the base of the depression and the pipe is complete. The user places a small quantity of herbal or resin cannabis in the depression and lights it whilst sucking at the ring pull opening. The body of the can being metal and large enough provides some cooling of the smoke. When finished the can is simply thrown away and a new one made when required.

As with all other cannabis paraphernalia, toke cans are available ready made and are often seen with hand-painted cannabis leaves decorating the sides and with a reinforced smoking bowl.

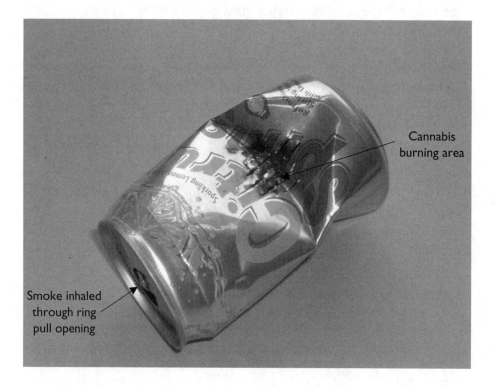

Cannabis burning area

Smoke inhaled through ring pull opening

Figure 1.9: Homemade toke can

Other smoking methods

Cannabis smokers have found all sorts of other ingenious ways to indulge in their pastime.

One way of smoking cannabis is called *hot knifing*. A knife is heated with a match or cigarette lighter until it is very hot and then pressed against some herbal cannabis or a piece of resin, which will immediately begin to smoulder. The smoke is collected with a cupped hand or using a funnel made from the top of a lemonade bottle, and breathed in. Another variation is to use two hot knives and to pick up a piece of cannabis resin between the blades, collecting the smoke as before. Yet another variation is known as *spotting*. A small piece of resin is impaled on the end of a pin; sometimes the pin at the back of a badge is used. The resin is then ignited with a match or lighter and the smoke allowed to fill a glass, often a beer glass. When full, the glass is passed around a group with each member 'drinking' some of the smoke.

Many web-based suppliers offers cannabis pipes that are disguised so that they appear to be something else. Many are made to look exactly like marker or fountain pens. We have also seen examples where a ceramic cigarette complete with filter tip and apparently burning tip has been made that houses within it a miniature cannabis pipe. The user loads it with a small amount of cannabis, lights it, and can then smoke their THC whilst others assume they are smoking tobacco.

A fairly common type is disguised to look like a car key. The smoking bowl is housed in the finger grip part of the key with a smoke path running to the tip of the metal part of the key.

Eating cannabis

Whilst smoking cannabis is by far the most popular method of using the drug, cannabis can be taken by mouth. Herbal or resin cannabis can be eaten on its own, but is more usually included as an ingredient in various forms of cooking. The drug can be introduced into all sorts of food items; pies, stews, pizzas, quiches and biscuits are very popular. Hash cakes containing the drug are regular fare at some parties. Many websites specialize in this branch of the cannabis scene and offer recipes and cooking advice covering a wide range of foods. Also available is a wide range of cannabis confectionary. Cannabis-laced sweets and lollypops, known as *fun candy* or *hemp suckers*, are to be found for sale at a large number of Internet 'head shops' and specialist confectionary websites. All of these products contain cannabis in various strengths and provide for the user all of the usual cannabis effects whilst they carry out the apparently innocent act of eating sweets.

Drinking cannabis

Cannabis can be mixed with spirit alcohol to produce a tincture. Many recipes for such a drink exist. Most recommend the use of herbal cannabis and a sweet-tasting spirit such as a fruit schnapps. The process of allowing the THC to dissolve into the alcohol takes several days, but produces a drink with the intoxication properties of both alcohol and cannabis combined. We recently came across a recipe for a drink called 'Green Dragon' made from herbal cannabis and vodka.

A drink can also be prepared by infusing herbal cannabis in boiling water to make a form of tea, also popular at parties. The potency of such a drink will be low, as THC does not dissolve in water and the drinker will only ingest that which remains suspended in the water. A stronger version can be made using cannabis that has previously been dissolved into butter, thus taking advantage of the fat soluble quality of THC, or by using milk instead of water for the same reason.

Taking the drug by eating or drinking introduces the THC into the bloodstream via the stomach and large intestine. This method is much slower than using the pulmonary capillaries, which is what smoking does, but once the THC has reached the bloodstream the effect is much the same, and longer lasting.

Notes

1   Spinella, M. (2005) *Concise Handbook of Psychoactive Herbs.* Binghampton, NY: Haworth Press.

2   Wachtel, S.R., ElSohly, M.A., Ross, S.A., Ambre, J. and de Wit, H. (2002) 'Comparison of the subjective effects of Delta(9)-Tetrahydrocannabinol and Marijuana in humans.' *Psychopharmacology 161,* 331–9. Δ is the Greek letter delta.

3   Julien, R.M. (2005) *A Primer of Drug Action: Tenth Edition.* New York: Worth Publishers.

Chapter Two

Cannabis and Health

Medicinal cannabis use

Neither of us can claim to be professional historians, and in preparing this brief history of medicinal cannabis use we have had to draw upon the published work of many others. As we did so, it quickly became apparent that there are many versions of such a history available to the interested reader. As a simple example of such variation, one has only to look at the start date for cannabis use by humans claimed in a small selection of such published 'histories'. The earliest claimed start date that we have read is that of 10,000 BCE,[1] although this author offers an alternative date of 6000 BCE later in the same volume. Other authors[2] opt for 8000 BCE, whilst a date some four millennia later seems to have found favour with a larger number of other authors.[3] In evidence presented to the UK Parliament in 1998,[4] a significantly later date of 600 BCE was given for humanity's first involvement with the drug. Little or no specific evidence is given by the authors in support of any of these dates, and the reader is left unable to be sure of what to trust. Perhaps in view of the high level of confusion and uncertainty surrounding the historical time line of cannabis use, authoritative drug authors such as Robert Julien[5] avoid quoting specific dates, particularly very early dates, by using such expressions as 'The use of cannabis sativa dates from several thousand years ago'. When we quote more precise dates, it is only when they are supported by evidence that is clear and unequivocal.

The use of cannabis has been linked with human culture for thousands of years. It is not surprising therefore that its many chemical properties and effects on the mind and body have been trialled and utilized medicinally throughout this time, to treat many physical and psychological problems, with varying degrees of success.

It is possible that the Chinese were the first to use cannabis for medicinal purposes, probably from as far back as 4000 BCE, and its use is known to have been recorded in a Chinese herbal dating from 2737 BCE. Another written account of its medical use by the Chinese, dating from the first century BCE, shows that it was used to treat diverse medical conditions such as rheumatism, muscle stiffness, inflammation and soreness, and even constipation and forgetfulness. This last affliction was thought to have been caused due to a lack of 'Yin' within the body. 'Yin' is thought to be responsible for feminine, negative and passive qualities, whereas its opposite, 'Yang', is responsible for masculine, positive and active qualities. Its use as a remedy for forgetfulness is surprising, as it is well known nowadays that cannabis can affect short-term memory,[6] although some users have reported that it can at times help them to focus better on what they are doing.

Staying with the Chinese, in the second century CE, extracts from the cannabis plant were used as an anaesthetic for abdominal surgery, particularly on the stomach and intestines, an area of the body that apparently was not favourably affected by acupuncture.

In India too some of the perceived medical qualities of cannabis were known, and, in a medical book pre-dating 1400 BCE, details of its effectiveness in treating anxiety were recorded, which would seem wholly reasonable considering the calming and mildly euphoric effects it can produce. Between the fifteenth and seventeenth century CE, physicians in India considered cannabis beneficial for the treatment of leprosy, and in ancient Hindu medicine it was employed as a sedative, to relieve constipation, asthma and rheumatic pains, and even as an appetite suppressant – which is somewhat bizarre as it is well documented today as an agent to promote appetite.[7]

Other civilizations/empires such as the Turks, Greeks and Egyptians were also aware of the properties of cannabis to affect the human body and mind, as were the Romans, with a clear description of the potential medicinal uses of cannabis being included in the *Materia Medica* written by the Greek physician Pedanius Dioscorides who was working in Rome circa 50–60 CE, and who recommended the use of cannabis to ease the pain of earache and in the treatment of jaundice.

In Europe, cannabis use has featured in the folk medicine of many countries, for example in Germany, where sprigs of the cannabis plant were laid directly on the body as an anticonvulsive treatment or for assisting with a difficult childbirth.

In 1792, Culpeper's *English Physician Enlarged*[8] described cannabis as: 'so well known to every good housewife, that I do not need to write any description of it'. Culpeper advocated the use of the plant for the treatment of headaches, stomach upsets and restlessness and as an aid to sleep. He advocated the use of the root of the plant in the treatment of inflammation, gout, hip pain and tumours. Indeed, it is well known that Queen Victoria used a cannabis preparation to relieve period pains. Her physician, Russell Reynolds, described it as: 'One of the most valuable therapeutic agents we possess.' Some medicinal preparations containing cannabis were still available in UK retail pharmacies up until 1973. Certain synthetically produced cannabinoid drugs are dispensed to patients nowadays, for a range of medical conditions, under names such as Nabilone, Dronabinol and Sativex™.

In Poland, Lithuania, Russia and the Ukraine, folk medicine commends inhaling the vapours given off when cannabis plant material is placed on hot stones, or the use of a cannabis-based porridge, in order to treat toothache. In the former Czechoslovakia, cannabis was sometimes utilized to treat wounds, and to reduce fever, whereas again in Russia cannabis seed oil has been employed in the treatment of jaundice and rheumatism.

Moving continents, and now particularly focusing on the US, the medicinal properties of cannabis are mentioned in medical notes from as far back as 1843,[9] and the plant was officially recommended for treatment of depression, gout, tetanus, insanity, hysteria and hydrophobia (rabies), with plant extracts even being prescribed to alleviate dysentery, a condition which became prevalent among soldiers of the Civil War period.

Right up until 1937, cannabis had been listed in US pharmacopoeia as a tranquillizing substance, although users were cautioned against the consumption of large amounts. Also at this time, Congress passed the Marijuana Tax Act, which heavily increased the purchase price of any product containing cannabis. However, cannabis continued to be widely utilized in patent medicines throughout the early part of the twentieth century, sometimes even being used to treat addiction to other drugs, such as opium. Then in 1941 the US government wholly removed approval for its use.

The use of cannabis for medical reasons in the twenty-first century

However, the use of cannabis for therapeutic purposes has persisted until the present time, and, worldwide, many promote its use, and believe in its properties for the benefits of health, mostly for the relief of unpleasant symptoms and side effects of certain illnesses or their treatments. Much of this is based on anecdotal evidence of its beneficial effects. Nevertheless, with so many and widespread supporters for its use for medical reasons, further research still needs to be undertaken to ensure that we are not depriving others in need of pain-killing and anti-emetic therapies, for example of a viable and possibly more effective alternative to currently available medications. In our own work with people with HIV, drug-related problems and certain other medical conditions, we have come across those who have extolled the virtues of cannabis use as a great benefit in the controlling of muscle pain, nausea, sleep problems and lack of appetite, and other unpleasant medical symptoms.

Before we move on to look at the range of conditions for which cannabis use is considered by many to be beneficial, we need to understand more about the active components of the plant, known as *cannabinoids*, what they are, how and where they are produced, what their function is, and how they act upon the body and brain.

Cannabinoids

Cannabinoids form a group of substances, some of which are found in the *Cannabis sativa* plant, including the psychoactive agent known as $\Delta 9$ Tetrahydrocannabinol (THC). Those found within the plants are known as *phyto-cannabinoids*, others that are naturally produced within the human body are known as *endo-cannabinoids*, whilst the third type, which can be produced chemically within a laboratory setting, are labelled the *synthetic cannabinoids*.

Phyto-cannabinoids are to be found mostly in the resinous sap exuded from gland-like structures on the leaves and flowering parts of the female cannabis plant. The male plant appears to have little or no THC content and its function is merely to fertilize the female.

To date, more than 60 different cannabinoids[10] have been identified within the plant, but the main ones we shall consider here are:

- THC – $\Delta 9$ Tetrahydrocannabinol

- CBD – Cannabidiol

- CBN – Cannabinol.

THC is the ingredient within the plant that has the effective psychoactive qualities desired mostly by recreational users. It acts upon certain receptor cells within the brain, known as CB1 and CB2[11] receptors which were first discovered in the late 1980s. The mildly euphoric effect is caused when THC binds with the CB1 receptors. Low-threshold pain-relieving qualities also come about as the result of this fusion. Selective breeding and cloning techniques have been introduced over the years to increase the THC content of certain plants, which are earmarked for recreational drug use, producing more potent varieties of street cannabis such as skunk and super-skunk, which therefore have a greater effect on the user.

Stimulation of the CB1 and CB2 receptors in the brain is facilitated by the production of yet another group of substances within the body known as endo-cannabinoids (for example Anandamide and 2-AD), and these act just like other neurotransmitters, such as dopamine, within the central nervous system.[12]

CBD, unlike THC, has no psychoactive properties, and binds mostly with CB2 receptors. It has a more physical effect on the body rather than psychological, and it thought to be an effective agent in the relief of such conditions as anxiety, nausea and sickness, and is also believed to have anti-inflammatory and anti-convulsive properties.

CBN is produced when THC starts to break down over time, so it is not very prevalent in freshly harvested plant material. The THC in cannabis in all its forms will gradually degrade, a process of oxidation which is quickened by exposure to the air or sunlight. As THC content reduces and CBN increases, the drug loses many of its psychoactive qualities, and is considered then to be more sedating rather than euphoric.

Cannabinoids, once ingested, are generally broken down in the body by the liver into *metabolites*, which are then excreted slowly. This is why cannabis use can sometimes be detected through urine sampling many weeks after it has been used.[13] Cannabinoids such as THC are fat soluble, and are absorbed into the lipid tissues of the body where they are retained for extended periods, before slowly passing back into the bloodstream to be metabolized and excreted. If cannabinoids were soluble in water, then their metabolites would be excreted from the body much quicker (in the same way as the metabolites of heroin and cocaine), and the window for detection of use would be much smaller.

A few synthetic cannabinoids have been manufactured for medicinal purposes, but as yet they are not widely available for general use. They include the following:

- *Dronabinol* (Marinol™), is used for pain relief, to stimulate appetite and as an anti-emetic.

- *Nabilone* (Cesamet™), is produced in capsule form and used for the relief of vomiting and nausea brought on by the toxic effects of chemotherapy for cancer treatment, especially where more conventional anti-emetics have proved ineffective. It is recommended that usage be observed and that it is given to hospital inpatients only, one reason being that drowsiness may occur affecting the patient's performance in carrying out skilled tasks such as driving, another being that the effects of alcohol are exacerbated.

- *Rimonabant* (Acomplia™, Zimulti™), is used as an anti-obesity drug and to help with cigarette smoking cessation.

- *Sativex*™, is produced as an oral spray, the usage of which is at present mostly restricted to Canada and Spain. It is used for the treatment of neuropathic pain and spasticity, especially for patients with multiple sclerosis. Although not currently licensed for use in the UK, it can be prescribed by doctors on a 'named patient' basis, but this is rare at present.

Much of the evidence of the beneficial effects of cannabis on a variety of medical conditions is still anecdotal. However, there can be little doubt, especially as we readily accept the medicinal effects of the synthetically produced cannabinoids, that further research needs to be undertaken to harness all the potential medical benefits cannabis could bring. This is even more true when you reflect back on how long it has been a part of human medical history.

Table 2.1 lists and describes a number of conditions for which people currently claim that cannabis can bring some relief,[14] although this list is by no means exhaustive. No doubt many further physical and psychological conditions exist for which cannabis use may prove to be beneficial. These may come to light with the growing interest apparent amongst certain members of the public and the increasing commercial research being undertaken by pharmaceutical companies to harness the pharmaceutical properties of cannabis and the financial profits these could bring.

Apart from the conditions already detailed in Table 2.1, further anecdotal evidence quotes cannabis as also being beneficial for the following health problems:

- muscle pain/tension

- nausea/sickness/vomiting

- restlessness/anxiety

- sleep disorders/insomnia

- eating disorders/appetite loss/anorexia/weight loss

- convulsions/seizures

- irritable bowel syndrome

- chronic heartburn

- neuralgia

- coughs

- strokes

- brain tumours

- menstrual cramps/period pains

- depression

- general pain

- post-operative pain (mostly neck, upper body, facial muscle)

- Tourette's syndrome.

In the majority of cases of claimed beneficial therapeutic use of cannabis, it is either smoked/inhaled or eaten. However, it is also used in poultices, mixed with alcohol as a tincture or included in creams or ointments for application to the skin, as appropriate.

This kind of usage is still illegal in most countries, although prosecutions are generally rare. Some prosecutions have resulted in acquittal following a defence of medical necessity. It still poses an ethical and moral dilemma, however, for those who see their cannabis use as essential to their state of health and well-being.

Possible problems

No psychoactive drug, whether it be legal, illegal or even prescribed, will ever be 100 per cent safe. There will always be some sort of side effect, no matter how small, an unwanted psychological or physical response, or even a total adverse or allergic reaction for some who use it. Cannabis therefore is no different to any other brain-altering drug in this respect.

In our discussions with a number of recreational users over the years, many have described to us minor problems that they have experienced when using cannabis, but appear to accept them as the occupational hazard of its use. Even medical users of the drug have disclosed to us that usage can cause further unwanted problems, but consider them of little consequence when compared with the benefits that they receive from using the drug.

Table 2.1: Medical conditions

Medical condition	Perceived benefits of cannabis
Glaucoma Raised intra-ocular pressure Damage to optic nerve Possible loss of eyesight	Reduction in intra-ocular pressure Protects optic nerve from damage
Multiple Sclerosis Incurable chronic disease of central nervous system Loss of muscular co-ordination Weakness, unsteadiness, muscle rigidity, tremor Incontinence	Reduction in muscle stiffness and spasms Relief of muscle and nerve pain, helps with sleep, bowel and bladder control, improvement in muscle co-ordination Helps with nausea, anxiety, depression, appetite loss, spasticity and tremors
HIV disease/AIDS Viral destruction of immune system Susceptibility to disease Incurable	Increases appetite in wasting syndrome Relieves nausea and sickness Helps with sleep, relieves anxiety and depression, promotes relaxation and calm Mild analgesic effects, helps with inflammatory gastric conditions Improves neuropathy, paresthesia, nerve and muscle pain
Arthritis Inflammation of joints with pain, swelling and restricted movement	Reduces pain, relaxes muscles allowing greater mobility, anti-inflammatory properties
Hypertension Abnormally high blood pressure Risk of kidney disease, stroke and heart attack	Slows heart beat, reducing blood pressure Removes anxiety and promotes calm
Epilepsy Fits/convulsions caused by abnormal electrical discharges between cerebral hemispheres	Decrease in number of seizures and blocking of convulsions

Table 2.1: Medical conditions *cont.*

Medical condition	Perceived benefits of cannabis
Huntington's Chorea Rare heredity disease of central nervous system Involuntary movements Emotional disturbance Mental deterioration leading to dementia Depression	Delay in the onset of symptoms Beneficial effect on involuntary movements of face muscles and limbs
Parkinson's Disease Degenerative brain disease Loss of mobility, muscle rigidity, tremors and speech difficulties	Relaxes muscles, reduces tremor Reduces side effects of conventional medicines used to treat the disease, e.g. insomnia, vomiting, muscle spasms and nausea Helps in movement disorder
Migraine Incapacitating headache Nausea, vision problems	Pain relief Promotes relaxation Stops nausea Aids sleep
Crohn's Disease Chronic inflammatory bowel disease Loss of appetite and weight loss Abdominal cramps, diarrhoea, fever	Improves appetite, reduces abdominal cramps Controls bowel movement Reduces pain
Asthma Chronic breathing condition Spasms in bronchial tubes which become inflamed	Reduces spasms, relaxes bronchial muscles, bronchodilatory effect
Diabetes Disorder of insulin production in body causing difficulties in regulating blood sugar levels	Lowers blood sugar levels for very short periods

The detrimental effects of cannabis use will be affected by a number of factors, some of which will be under the user's control, whilst others will not. These factors include:

- the type of cannabis being used and its strength
- which method of use is employed
- whether other substances are used at the same time
- the mood of the user
- how much is used at any one time
- whether any physical or psychological problems already exist
- the excretion time of the drug from the body (its half-life)
- the experience and expectations of the user
- whether there are any adulterants in the drug.

The type of cannabis used may merely be dependent on what is available at the time, or the finance available for its purchase.

Herbal cannabis (marijuana, weed, grass) has a lower THC level generally than the resin form (hash), and this in turn is surpassed by cannabis oil (hash oil, diesel), which generally has the highest THC content due to its method of manufacture.

With selectively bred plants and cloned varieties, such as those used to produce skunk and super-skunk, the THC content of the drug is much higher than plain herbal cannabis, and can easily catch out the new or naïve user or the unwary, due to its potency.

In common with users of other types of drugs, there will be a small percentage of cannabis users who are ultra-sensitive to its effects. Indeed, we have met many such people who stated their wish to join in with their friends and use cannabis, but who suffered very unpleasant side effects each time they did so. It is to be hoped that such people will realize at an early stage that the drug just does not suit them, and therefore curtail its use altogether. This applies also to those who have an existing physical or mental health problem such as bronchitis, emphysema, schizophrenia or psychosis. Such people really should consider avoiding cannabis altogether due to its psychoactive nature, and the many irritants to the respiratory system found amongst the tars and carcinogenic compounds found in its smoke.[15]

The following list[16] details the often-quoted, common health problems, risks and possible unpleasant side effects that should be considered by all those who wish to use cannabis, and that seem to be prevalent amongst many long-term existing users:

- paranoid feelings

- confusion

- panic attacks

- bizarre thoughts and constant questioning whilst under the influence

- hallucinations and delusions

- agitation (sometimes severe)

- problems with short-term memory

- lack of concentration and inability to process information

- changes in perception of time and space

- exacerbation of low mood/depression

- slowing of reaction time

- amotivational syndrome, leading to poor hygiene, poor diet and decrease in sense of responsibility

- adverse effects on judgement (e.g. distance and speed)

- depersonalization

- tar content higher than commercial cigarette tobacco

- higher number of carcinogenic compounds

- greater dangers when used with tobacco

- burns at a higher temperature than tobacco and can adversely affect the mucus membrane of the mouth, oesophagus, bronchus, etc. and damage the small hairs (cilia) of the respiratory tract, which help to trap and remove inhaled particulate matter

- dry mouth

- an initial increase in heart rate and workload on the heart which may increase the danger of an angina attack in sufferers

- disruption of menstruation and ovulation in females

- reduces testosterone levels and sperm production in males; also decreases the ability of sperm to move vigorously

- suppresses white blood cells, adversely affecting the ability of immune system to protect the body against diseases and infection

- can cross the placental barrier into bloodstream of foetus, and can also be passed through breast milk; this can result in foetal growth retardation, some abnormalities, premature birth, low birth weight and poor development of children

- potential for psychological addiction and some physical withdrawal symptoms

- development of tolerance, necessitating greater use of drug to achieve desired effect, which in turn affects cost and increases likelihood of health problems

- accumulates in fatty tissues of body (e.g. brain and testes) and therefore can continue to affect body function after use; may take weeks to be fully excreted and is detectable for long periods as a result

- adverse effects on balance and stability

- can cause sickness and vomiting if used with alcohol; exacerbates the effects of alcohol when used together

- dilates blood vessels in cornea, causing characteristic red eye

- reduces muscle strength and co-ordination.

Many of the above effects may be short-lived, and will disappear once cannabis use ceases, but for an unfortunate few, and particularly some chronic long-term users of cannabis, this is not always the case, as more permanent physical and psychological damage may have taken place.

The health implications of different methods of use

The health risks associated with cannabis use do not just come from the drug itself. Obviously the amount and type used, whether herbal, resin or oil, and the type of plant from which it has been manufactured, will determine the level of THC the user is exposed to, but the method of use can also bring further problems, so must be considered carefully in order to minimize potential harm.

Hand-rolled cigarettes

Smoking cannabis in a cigarette (joint) is the most prevalent methods of use. Commonly, tobacco is added to the mix, which increases the health risk, as both substances contain carcinogenic compounds in their smoke.

With a joint, the burning material is only a short 'roach distance' from the lips mouth and tongue, and so the very hot smoke has little opportunity to cool before entering the respiratory system, and thus can cause damage.

The use of a roach rather than a cigarette filter (which is believed by many users to reduce the amount of THC available to be inhaled in the smoke) also means that burnt particulates and tar deposits are free to enter the lungs.

The size of the joint can also cause problems due to the amount of burnt cigarette paper particles that is inhaled, which could potentially add to the harm. Some users have told us that smaller joints equal less paper and thus fewer potential problems. However, an opposite view is also held by other users, who believe that a large and loosely packed joint reduces the burn temperature and is therefore preferable.

Coloured or flavoured cigarette papers should also be avoided, as the flavourings and dyes used will enter the respiratory tract once burned.

Smoking is, however, the quickest way for the THC and other cannabinoids to enter the bloodstream, via the lungs, and so the effects will come on sooner, thus allowing the user to better gauge their degree of intoxication or symptom relief, and help prevent overindulgence or some unwanted effects.

Water pipes

Because bhongs and other water pipes are designed to cool the hot cannabis smoke prior to inhalation, some users believe that this is a safer method of smoking the drug. However, this is open to discussion. It seems likely that a good percentage of the THC content of the smoke may actually be absorbed by the water itself,[17] necessitating a longer smoke to achieve the desired effects, thus increasing the level of tar inhaled. Rather than decreasing harm, this could actually increase the potential for damage to physical health, although some of the burnt particulate matter would be filtered out by the water.

Similarly, any methods utilized that cool the smoke so that it can be taken deeper into the lungs, and then held there for a longer duration, was thought to increase the THC absorption into the blood via the lungs, but this too is now being questioned, with the added concern that the deeper and longer the smoke is held there, the greater the potential for carcinogens and burnt particles in the smoke to do their worst.

Other potential problems concerning the use of water pipes can arise from their construction. Many people fashion their own bhongs from materials readily available around the house, utilizing plastic bottles, rubber and plastic piping, wooden tubes, aluminium foil, bottle tops and industrial sealant tape, for example. The high temperatures generated by use may make these items break down, releasing more potentially harmful contaminants into the smoke being inhaled.[18] Better-quality water pipes, commercially produced and currently available for purchase, tend to be made from glass or ceramics, with piping of steel or brass to minimize these types of problems.

Toke cans

Using a toke can is a quick and simple way to smoke cannabis. The body of a ring pull can will help to decrease the temperature of the smoke to a small extent, by dissipating the heat generated. The aluminium of which many of these cans are made, however, may be problematic when heated,[19] as may any paint on the outside of the can. One point in favour of choosing this method is that tobacco need not be used. However, nothing is filtered out from the smoke, leaving tars and carcinogens to enter the lungs.

Lungs

These devices are generally used when only small amounts of cannabis are available, as the majority of the smoke produced is captured, rather than being dispersed into the atmosphere. This method is also utilized by some who cannot afford or tolerate the use of tobacco. Once again the construction of the device can be problematic in itself due to the use of plastic bottles and bags, and aluminium foil or bottle tops on which to burn the cannabis. Smoke is likely to cool a little whilst in the 'bag' part of the lung, allowing some tar to condense, but no particulate matter is filtered out.

Vaporizers

This is an economical and safer[20] way of heating cannabis for inhaling. If used correctly, the operator can ensure that the cannabis is heated rather than burned, releasing THC as a vapour, and not as smoke. This is because THC is released as a vapour at a lower temperature than the ignition point of the plant matter, resulting in a cooler 'smoke' with significantly less in the way of burnt particles. However, a fine dust may still be present within the vapour. The lower temperature vapour is better for the lungs than is the higher temperature smoke of burnt cannabis. However, if the vaporizer is overheated, then the experience is just as it would be for smoking the drug, with all the resultant toxins, irritants and carcinogenic compounds being inhaled.

Chillum pipes

These are pipes made from metal, ceramic, glass or other materials, usually with a long smoke path which are designed to cool the smoke from burning cannabis, reducing damage to the sensitive lining of the mouth, oesophagus and lungs. As with toke cans and joints, none of the smoke is filtered, allowing particulate matter to enter the lungs.

Bear hugging

There appear to be two different methods of inhaling cannabis smoke both called 'bear hugging' and these appear to be popular with young males especially, as part of cannabis 'party games'.

One variation of 'bear hugging' was described to us by several users. This is where the smoker is grabbed from behind by another person who squeezes them very tightly to expel as much air as possible out of the smoker's lungs. Then, before inhaling commences, a joint, bhong or lung is placed in the smoker's mouth, so that, once a breath is taken, only cannabis smoke will enter the respiratory system. Users of this method report feeling 'stoned' almost immediately, but this may not be a direct result of the drug itself, but may be caused by a momentary lack of oxygen to the brain (anoxia). This method of cannabis use is also dangerous because the concentrated smoke is taken very deep into the lungs.

The second variation is best described using the exact words of a contributor to a cannabis users website.[21]

> To get this right, you have to be REALLY stoned in the first place... Put your head between your legs and take a REALLY really hard toke, bending back upwards as you toke. Breathe in as much as your lungs will hold. As you reach the top, get somebody to come over and give you the equivalent of a bear hug. They have to make sure they press HARD on your chest (not so hard as to break anything). At the same time (if you don't black out instantly) hold your nose and close your mouth so's you're airtight, and then cough. You should black out and have really intense dreams for about 30 seconds.

> Don't do this without friends (even if you just try the coughing part), the chances are you'll fall and wake up hardly [sic] remembering anything (this lasts about a minute).

The potential for harm using the method as described above is self-evident.

Eating cannabis

Using cannabis as an ingredient in foodstuffs avoids the many problems associated with inhaling its smoke or vapour. The effects of cannabis when eaten in food come on more steadily than if it is smoked, taking anything up to an hour[22] to begin, but then last longer, up to 10 or 12 hours. Because of the indeterminate dosage when adding it to food, it is possible to consume too much, resulting in over-intoxication. However, another problem that could arise from this method of use can be linked to the type of cannabis used. To maximize profits, manufacturers and suppliers will adulterate cannabis – like other street drugs – with all manner of unhealthy material, some of which will survive the cooking process[23] and be potentially very dangerous to the user.

The problems outlined above will also apply when cannabis is used as an ingredient in drinks.

Application directly to the skin

For medical purposes, lotions, creams and tinctures can easily be manufactured for application directly to the skin or for use in poultices. The active ingredients can then be absorbed through the skin. No additional problems arise from this method of use, only those associated with the drug itself.

Adulterants

In January 2007, the UK Department of Health[24] issued a warning to all drug services to inform their clients that cannabis had been found containing small silica beads and ground glass particles which, when smoked, could potentially cause harm to the user. Similar official warnings were issued by the French Department of Health later in 2007,[25] and people who had smoked this type of adulterated cannabis were advised to see a doctor as a precaution, as their lungs could be damaged. Indeed, in France, it seems that some people have been hospitalized for this very reason. The adulterated cannabis was thought to have originated in Taiwan, where it was known that reflective road surfacing material was being used as a cannabis bulking agent. However, it is well known that certain types of cannabis contain more harmful substances than others, and so the more health-conscious user needs to be aware of the more notorious kinds, such as 'soap bar', 'grit grass', 'superweed' and 'squidgy black'.

Besides the glass particles discussed above the following potentially harmful adulterants have been found in certain batches of cannabis.[26]

Animal faeces	Garden herbs	Phencyclidine
Aspirin	Glues	Pine resin
Barbiturates	Grasses	Salt
Beeswax	Grit	Sand
Benzene	Ground coffee	Stock cubes
Boot polish	Henna	Sugars
Dyes	Ketamine	Toluene
Engine oil	Milk powder	Turpentine
Fibre glass	Mud	

Dependent upon the type of cannabis being offered, many other substances could be mixed with it, including other legal, prescribed or illegal drugs, all kinds of powdered materials, and any other kind of plant detritus.

In fact, we have even encountered a self-styled dealer some years ago who was offering 'grass' to young people near a secondary school which, when analyzed, was shown to be exactly that, grass cut from someone's lawn! The dealer, therefore, could not even be prosecuted under any consumer legislation. After all, he told his potential customers exactly what they were buying.

Expectations and mood of user

One long-term cannabis user with whom we have dealt over the years was at one point in his life very badly burned from the waist down in a road traffic accident. Due to the injuries to his legs, he found it very difficult to walk without agonizing pain. However, he told us that before getting out of bed in the morning he would smoke one or two 'joints', resulting in a reduction in his pain levels, and relaxation of his leg muscles, which then allowed him to move more easily.

When we discussed the possibility of transferring him to a prescribed medicinal form of cannabinoid, he politely declined, stating that he believed it would not be as effective, as for so many years he had associated the ritual of constructing and smoking his joint, with relaxation and analgesia, a form of self-induced Pavlovian classical conditioning. Thus the action of taking a pill, capsule or oral spray would not give him the confidence he needed in the drug's medicinal properties.

This is actually not an unusual occurrence, as many users become familiar with using the drug in a particular way that they have become comfortable with.

Mood can also be a factor in how the user perceives the effect of the drug. Although cannabis may initially seem to enhance mood, rather like alcohol, it may then go on to accentuate the existing mood of the user, making those who are feeling down even more depressed.

Notes

1   Green, J. (2002) *Cannabis: The Hip History of Hemp* London: Pavilion Books.

2   Earleywine, M. (2005) *Understanding Marijuana*. Oxford: Oxford University Press; Nordegren, T. (2002) *The A-Z Encyclopaedia of Alcohol and Drug Abuse*. Boca Raton: Universal Publishers.

3   Brown, D. (1998) *Cannabis: The Genus Cannabis*. London: CRC Press; Rubin, V. (1975) *Cannabis and Culture*. The Hague: Moutan; Spinella, M. (2005) *Concise Handbook of Psychoactive Herbs*. Binghampton, NY: Haworth Press.

4   *Select Committee on Science and Technology: Ninth Report* (1998). London: Hansard.

5   Julien, R.M. (2005) *A Primer of Drug Action: Tenth Edition*. New York: Worth Publishers, pp.557.

6   Julien, R.M. (2005) *A Primer of Drug Action*. New York: Worth Publishers.

7   Croxford, J.L. (2003) 'Therapeutic potential of cannabinoids in CNS disease.' *CNS Drugs 17*, 179–202.

8   Culpeper, N. (1792) *The English Physician Enlarged: With Three Hundred and Sixty Nine Medicines Made of English Herbs, that Were Not in Any Impression Unit Until This*. London: J. Scatcherd.

9   Wood, G.B. and Bache, F. (1843) *The Dispensatory of the United States of America*. Philadelphia, PA: Grigg and Elliot.

10   Grotenhermen, F. and Russo, E. (2002) *Cannabis and Cannabinoids: Pharmacology, Toxicology, and Therapeutic Potential*. Binghampton: Haworth Press.

11   Pertwee, R.G. (2008) 'The diverse CB1 and CB2 receptor pharmacology of three plant cannabinoids: D9-tetrahydrocannabinol, cannabidiol and D9-tetrahydrocannabivarin.' *British Journal of Pharmacology 153*, 199–215.

12   Julien, R.M. (2005) *A Primer of Drug Action*. New York: Worth Publishers.

13   Center for Human Reliability Studies (2007) *Drug Retention Times*. Oak Ridge, TN: Oak Ridge Institute for Science and Education.

14   UK Independent Drug Monitoring Unit (IDMU); Grotenhermen, F. and Russo, E. (2002) *Cannabis and Cannabinoids: Pharmacology, Toxicology, and Therapeutic Potential*. Binghampton, NY: Haworth Press (available at www.idmu.co.uk/canfaq.htm, accessed 21 August 2008).

15   Julien, R.M. (2005) *A Primer of Drug Action*. New York: Worth Publishers.

16   Centre for Addiction and Mental Health (2003) 'Cannabis: Do you know...' Toronto, Canada: Centre for Addiction and Mental Health; Tashkin, D.P. (1999) 'Effects of marijuana on the lung and its defences against cancer and infection.' *School Psychology International 20*, 1, 23–37; National Institute on Drug Abuse (2005) *Marijuana Abuse*. Bethesda, MD: National Institute on Drug Abuse; American Society for Biochemistry and Molecular Biology, press release 26 April 2006; British Lung Foundation, London, press release 31 July 2007.

17   Gieringer, D. (1996) 'Marijuana water pipe and vaporizer study.' *Newsletter of the Multidisciplinary Association for Psychedelic Studies 6*, 3, summer.

18   UK Cannabis Internet Activists (UKCIA). '*Risk of getting stoned – how you do it*' (available at www.ukcia.org/culture/effects/how2.htm, accessed 12 February 2007).

19 *Ibid.*

20 The National Organization for the Reform of Marijuana Laws (NORML) (2007) '"Smokeless" cannabis delivery system found "safe and effective", study says.' NORML, 19 April (available at http://norml.org/index.cfm?Group_ID=7240, accessed 13 February 2008).

21 Marijuana.Com (available at www.marijuana.com/games-sports/42844-weed-party-games.html, accessed 13 March 2008).

22 Drake, B. (2002) *Marijuana Food Handbook*. Oakland, CA: Ronin Publishing.

23 UK Cannabis Internet Activists (UKCIA) *Guide to Eating Cannabis* (available at www.ukcia.org/culture/eat.php, accessed 13 February 2008).

24 Department of Health UK (2007) 'Contamination of herbal or 'skunk-type cannabis with glass beads.' (available at www.info.doh.gov.uk/doh/embroadcast.nsf/vwDiscussionAll/297D9740D0412C9D802572650050A4A0?OpenDocument, accessed 13 February 2008).

25 Ministry of Health France (2007) "Alerte à l'herbe coupée aux microbilles!" 9 March (available at www.circ-asso.net/paris/pages/alerte.htm, accessed 13 February 2008).

26 Cannabis Campaign Guide 'Warning: fibre-glass laced bud in the UK.' (available at www.ccguide.org.uk/badsoap.php, accessed 13 February 2008).

Chapter Three

Cannabis and Mental Health – Looking at the Research

Much new information has appeared over the past few years indicating that the use of cannabis can have a considerably detrimental effect on mental health and functioning. Indeed, this is a fact that has been known for over 150 years, but, more specifically, this new information has been linking the drug with the onset of major mental disorders such as psychosis and schizophrenia. Many peer-reviewed professional and scientific journals have published the results of cannabis use research carried out all over the world, and the popular press/ newspapers have been quick to pass this on to a wider audience, sometimes with sensational headlines. One such headline stated that 500 people per week were hospitalized in the UK due to cannabis abuse.[1]

A number of television programmes on this subject, together with many health-focused leaflets and websites, have been produced worldwide. Several of these are aimed especially at the younger cannabis user, as much of the research claims that the earlier the commencement of cannabis use the greater the potential problems for the user in later life.

In this chapter we look at a few of these research studies and their findings, and the views of highly respected and learned key players who have helped to draw this important information to our attention.

Before we start our exposition of these research studies, it is important that we clarify our understanding of some of the mental conditions that these research studies refer to.

Definitions

Schizophrenia

Schizophrenia is a serious mental disorder which can result in profound changes to a patient's personality, perception and behaviour. Symptoms are very varied and described as either 'positive' (the acute syndrome) or 'negative' (the chronic syndrome).

Table 3.1: Symptoms of schizophrenia

Positive symptoms	Negative symptoms
Preoccupation, inactivity, withdrawal	Lack of drive, social withdrawal
Restlessness, inconsistency	Reduced speech
Mood changes (depression, anxiety, euphoria, irritation)	Abnormal movement
	Disorder of thought, blunting, stupor
Blunting (reduction in variations in mood)	Depression
Incongruity (emotions not in keeping with situation)	Overexcitement, incongruity, delusions, hallucinations (mostly auditory)
Thought disorders, vagueness	Persecutory feelings
Hallucinations (auditory, visual, tactile, olfactory)	Neglect of personal hygiene and appearance
Delusions, impaired attention and insight	

It may also be useful to outline a few pertinent facts regarding schizophrenia.[2]

- Around 1 in 100 of the population will experience a schizophrenic episode at some time in their lives.

- It appears to affect more men than women.

- It is rare for it to occur before the age of 15 years, and it most commonly occurs between the ages of 15 and 35 years.

- Around 1 in 7 schizophrenia sufferers will also experience depression.

- Schizophrenics are more liable to die sooner than the average member of the population.

- 20 per cent of sufferers will get better within five years of their first episode of schizophrenia.

- 60 per cent of sufferers will get better, but will still have some symptoms. They will have times when their symptoms get worse.

- 20 per cent of sufferers will continue to have troublesome symptoms.

- There is a higher suicide rate amongst schizophrenics than in the general population.

- Some people have a higher genetic probability of developing schizophrenia.

Psychosis

Psychosis is a broad term used to describe severe mental disorders where people may lose sight of reality without realizing they are unwell. It can include hallucinations and delusions and lack of insight. Psychosis is the term used prior to more precise symptoms being observed and recognized, when the diagnosis can be made more precisely.

Depression

This is an emotional state characterized by sadness, unhappy thoughts, apathy and dejection. The feeling of depression is much more powerful and unpleasant than the short episodes of unhappiness that we all experience from time to time. It goes on for much longer. It can last for months rather than days or weeks. Most people with depression will not have all the symptoms listed here,[3] but most will have at least five or six and will:

- feel unhappy most of the time (but may feel a little better in the evenings)

- lose interest in life and can't enjoy anything

- find it harder to make decisions

- be unable to cope with things that they used to

- feel utterly tired

- feel restless and agitated

- lose appetite and weight (some people find they do the reverse and put on weight)

- take one or two hours to get off to sleep, and then wake up earlier than usual

- lose interest in sex

- lose self-confidence

- feel useless, inadequate and hopeless

- avoid people

- feel irritable

- feel worse at a particular time each day, usually in the morning

- have suicidal thoughts.

We will now look at a small number of research studies that have looked at the issue of cannabis use and mental health.

Study one

Andréasson, S., Allbeck, P., Engström, A. and Rydberg, U. (1987) 'Cannabis and schizophrenia: A longitudinal study of Swedish conscripts.' *The Lancet 330*, 1483–5.

This was one of the first research studies to suggest a link between the use of cannabis and mental health problems in the long term.

The researchers utilized almost the total cohort of young men who had carried out their national service in the Swedish Army between 1969 and 1970. A total of 50,087 conscripts were interviewed, which made up 97 per cent of the 18–20-year-old male population at that time. Their individual health records were analyzed, and then followed up until the mid 1980s, in order to establish the number of cannabis users admitted into hospital with a diagnosis of schizophrenia during the 15-year period, as compared with the number of non-users also admitted for the same condition.

The data gathered demonstrated a significant association between cannabis usage throughout the formative teenage years, and the onset and incidence of schizophrenia in later life. Indeed, the research team concluded that, over the 15-year period, the young conscripts who had used cannabis prior to being called up for national service were six times more likely to be hospitalized with a diagnosis of schizophrenia than their non-using peers. This was particularly so for those who had reported use of cannabis on 50 or more occasions.

This association did not, however, imply that cannabis use was the cause of schizophrenia, merely that it was a factor in its onset.

There was some initial criticism of this research study as no differentiation could be made as to whether people with a predisposition to mental illness were more likely to use cannabis for recreational purposes (common factor explanation), or for self-medicating symptomatic relief (reverse causality), or whether the act of using cannabis led to the onset of schizophrenia.

Study two

Moore, T., Zammit, S., Lingford-Hughes, A., Barnes, T., Jones, P., Burke, M. and Lewis, G. (2007) 'Cannabis use and the risk of psychotic or affective mental health outcomes: A systematic review.' *The Lancet 370*, 319–28.

Over 4000 studies and reports from all over the world were considered in this comprehensive review, this being then whittled down to just 35 longitudinal population-based studies which met the researchers' exacting criteria. Extraction of the data, and quality control measures to ensure the reliability of that data, was carried out independently and then repeated to ensure accuracy. Adjustments were made where relevant to filter out any possible reverse causality effects.

The research team, after consideration of the pooled data, concluded that for people who had ever used cannabis there was a consistent increase of around one and a half times in the incidence of psychosis, and that this increased risk of a psychotic episode was around 40 per cent for such users. For regular heavy users of the drug (at least weekly), most of the studies included showed an increase in this risk of between 50 per cent and 200 per cent.

Working on recent estimated figures that showed that up to 40 per cent of adolescents in the UK have used cannabis at some time, and then considering that ever using cannabis can increase the risk of psychosis occurring by one and a half times, the team estimated that up to 14 per cent of psychotic episodes in young people could be prevented if cannabis use was removed from the equation.

The research team firmly believe that we have now had sufficient good-quality data driven evidence to support a warning to all young users and potential cannabis users, of the very real dangers they face in developing a psychotic illness later in their lives. As the drug is currently so prevalent in the lives of young people especially, the team also consider that cannabis use can be expected to be seen as a substantial factor in future psychotic disorders at a population level, and that the more frequent the use of cannabis, the greater the risk to the user.

Study three

Arseneault, L., Cannon, M., Poulton, R., Murrary, R., Caspi, A. and Moffit, T. (2002) 'Cannabis use in adolescence and risk for adult psychosis: Longitudinal prospective study.' *British Medical Journal 325*, 1212–13.

This study, carried out in Dunedin, New Zealand, included in its team the highly respected Professor Robin Murray of the Maudsley Hospital in London. The study followed the mental health of a cohort of 1037 people born in 1972/3 up until they reached the age of 26 years, with 96 per cent of the sample completing the study. Information was gathered on those who had already experienced psychotic symptoms by age 11 years, and self-reported drug use at ages 15 and 18 years and then, using standardized interview schedules, all were assessed at age 26 years for psychiatric symptoms. Analysis was carried out on a representative group of 759 individuals (74% of the cohort) for whom comprehensive data existed covering their adolescent use of illegal drugs, whether or not they had experienced any psychotic symptoms in early childhood, and for whom complete records concerning their psychiatric outcomes as adults were also available.

This group was further divided into smaller groups based on the age of cannabis use, whether at age 15 or 18 years. A control group of 494 individuals had reported no use of cannabis or use just once or twice, at both ages. Those who reported using cannabis three or more times at age 15 years had continued to use the drug right up until they were aged 18 years.

The psychiatric outcomes by age 26 years included schizophrenia and depressive symptoms, and diagnosis of schizophrenia-like disorder and depression.

Results showed that more schizophrenic symptoms had been experienced by cannabis users who had started their cannabis use at 15 or 18 years than those in the control group, and that the effects were stronger the earlier the drug was first used. This increase remained significant even when account was taken of those with a history of psychosis before the age of 11.

The team concluded that using cannabis during adolescence significantly increased the risk of experiencing schizophrenic symptoms later in life. If cannabis use started by age 18 years, users were 1½ more likely to experience psychosis by age 26 years, and that this likelihood rose to 4½ times if commencement was at age 15 years. The younger the cannabis user, the greater the risk also, because their use might become longstanding.

Study four

Patton, G., Coffey, C., Carlin, J., Degenhardt, L., Lynskey, M. and Hall, W. (2002) 'Cannabis use and mental health in young people: Cohort study.' *British Medical Journal 325*, 1195–8.

Many of the studies concerning the issue of cannabis and mental health problems in young people have concentrated on episodes of psychotic symptoms and schizophrenia. This Australian study, however, looked at other kinds of mental health disorders, namely depression and anxiety, which can still have a major impact on the lives of those who experience them.

This research team's objective was to determine whether adolescent cannabis use led to a greater incidence of anxiety and depression in later adulthood. The six-year study was carried out in seven waves, and involved secondary school students aged 14 to 15 years at the outset, from 44 state schools in the Australian state of Victoria. The total initially sampled was 2032 students, with nearly 96 per cent of them completing the first six waves of the study. This reduced to 79 per cent for Wave Seven due to attrition.

The study addressed three specific questions:

- Does cannabis use by adolescents act as a predictor of depression and anxiety in young adulthood?

- Do depression and anxiety lead to cannabis use in young adults?

- Do factors such as family background or use of other substances play a part?

Fourteen common psychiatric symptoms were considered with a total score of 12 or more of them being regarded as evidence of a depression or anxiety state that would be appropriate for some kind of clinical intervention. Cannabis use was assessed as either never used, used less than weekly, used weekly and used daily (five or more days each week). The team also made assessments of participants' use of tobacco, alcohol and other illicit drugs.

Results showed that 66 per cent of males and 52 per cent of females in the study self-reported use of cannabis at some time, and that 75 per cent of these had begun using the drug as teenagers; 10 per cent of young males and 4 per cent of young females were considered as daily users, whilst 20 per cent of males and 8 per cent of females were using weekly.

Daily use of cannabis by young females was associated with odds of over five times that of non-users for the onset of depression and anxiety in later life. Weekly use of the drug in the teens of young females predicted a doubling of the possibility of depression and anxiety occurring, rising to a fourfold increase if use had been daily.

Depression in teenagers, however, was not a predictor of a higher degree of cannabis usage. Self-medication of symptoms with cannabis was considered, but no relation between adolescent depression and anxiety and later use of cannabis was found.

The team concluded that frequent cannabis usage among teenage females was a predictor for later onset depression and anxiety, with the greatest degree of risk being carried by daily users of the drug.

Study five

Van Os, J., Bak, M., Hanssen, M., Bijl, R., de Graaf, R. and Verdoux, H. (2002) 'Cannabis use and psychosis: A longitudinal population-based study.' *American Journal of Epidemiology 156*, 319–27.

This three-year follow-up study (1997/98/99) was carried out in the Netherlands, where cannabis is widely accepted as a recreational drug, and where the authorities turn a blind eye to personal use; thus the reporting of cannabis use would not place the participants in any danger of conflict with the law and legal proceedings.

The aims were to try and establish whether use of cannabis independently increased the risk of experiencing a psychosis, taking into account other substance use, and whether those who already had a predisposed vulnerability to psychosis were placing themselves at greater risk by using the drug.

A random sampling procedure was used, and a total of 7076 participants identified at the baseline. Participants were interviewed by lay interviewers at home, with the response rate at commencement of 69.7 per cent. All those who had demonstrated significant psychotic symptoms at baseline interview were re-interviewed by an experienced clinician (47.2%) and again at second interview (74.4%) due to the relevance of their symptoms. The final assessment interviews took place in 1999. At second interview 5618 participants took part, and at the third and final interview 4848 took part. Full assessments of other substance use was also made, and taken into account during all three assessment periods.

Of the 4045 participants who at baseline interview showed a lifetime absence of psychotic symptoms to that date, seven went on to develop them by the time of the third assessment interviews. Psychosis was reported by 38 participants at the third assessment interview, and those with this outcome had previously shown higher cannabis use levels at the baseline.

Overall the study showed that, at baseline assessment, those who already had a history of cannabis use but with absence of psychosis were placing themselves at increased risk of a psychotic outcome later on. This baseline lifetime history of cannabis use was also shown to be a greater predictor of psychotic outcome than use of cannabis and other substances over the follow-up period. Those at baseline who had been reported as having an established vulnerability to psychotic episodes were also shown as becoming even more vulnerable if they used cannabis.

The research team therefore concluded that the study had demonstrated that use of cannabis is an independent risk factor in the onset of psychotic symptoms, particularly for those already with an established vulnerability and therefore for whom use of the drug could result in a poor outcome.

Summing up the research

After reviewing the research evidence, there is no doubt that cannabis can and does play a significant part in the onset of mental health problems for some, but especially for those with an underlying predisposition to such illnesses, or those who have already experienced such disorders.

Indeed, a poll of 50 of the world's leading authorities on drug misuse and mental health, carried out in 2007,[4] confirmed that most are of the opinion that use of cannabis, especially the modern stronger varieties, poses significant mental health risks to users. However, these conclusions are still being disputed by some medical experts and by an even greater number of cannabis users around the world who personally have encountered little or no mental health difficulties that they attribute to their use of the drug, save perhaps for some paranoia.

To complete our review of the links between cannabis use and mental health problems, we sought the views on this issue of two consultant psychiatrists in the UK, one working in the field of substance misuse and the other working in the field of adult mental health. We have worked closely with these two eminent consultants for many years, and place great value on their views, opinions and specialized knowledge.

Dr Sidney Hettiaratchy is a Fellow of the Royal College of Psychiatrists and has been working as a consultant in the field of child and adolescent mental health since 1975, and as a consultant in substance misuse since 1985. He told us:

Cannabis is commonly regarded as an innocuous drug. Such a belief has been fostered by the misunderstanding that followed the reclassification of cannabis. However it is now commonly agreed amongst doctors that cannabis use can be an important factor in some people's mental health. Although it is agreed that smoking cannabis in itself does not cause mental illness, those people who are predisposed to psychoses are much more likely to develop symptoms if they use the drug regularly. Many of these effects are dose related, but constitutional factors such as age, personality attributes and vulnerability to mental illness may also play a part. In some users, cannabis can lead to a range of short-lived symptoms such as depersonalization, derealization, a feeling of loss of control, irrational panic and paranoid ideas. Such symptoms may remit on abstinence. Others users can experience symptoms such as hearing of voices or having unwarranted feelings of persecution or risk of harm from others. These symptoms may persist after abstinence. Such a presentation can be associated with heavy cannabis use, particularly with the stronger varieties, and resemble a functional illness similar to acute schizophrenia. A link between cannabis use and depression has also been addressed in recent research. Overall, the evidence suggests that regular cannabis use is associated with increased levels of depression or depressive symptoms. Young people who use cannabis, particularly at an early age, are at greater risk of experiencing adverse effects than those who begin using in later adolescence or early adulthood. Both educational achievement and mental health may be compromised.

Dr Hettiaratchy concluded by saying, 'Young people in general urgently need to be better informed as to the risks cannabis use poses to their mental and physical health'.

Our second consultant, Dr John Rees, who specializes in adult mental health, agreed with all the points made by his colleague, adding that when dealing with young adults with schizophrenia and other serious mental health problems their treatment was sometimes compromised when their use of cannabis continued, prolonging the duration of their illness, and jeopardizing a successful outcome.

To complement the opinions of these two consultant psychiatrists, we also asked a British doctor with 14 years in general practice what experience he had of patients presenting with health problems associated with their cannabis use. This GP, who wished to remain unnamed, described the mix of patients on his list as 'broad in terms of age, sex and social economic group'. He went on to say:

My experience of patients presenting with cannabis-related physical or mental health issues is that it usually occurs in predominantly young men from mid teens through to early forties. We do see some cannabis use in women of course. However, my experience of this suggests that this is not such a large problem.

Patients rarely seek advice for cannabis-related physical illnesses. Most cannabis users we come across are also smokers and it is difficult to distinguish between any chronic obstructive airways disease due to cannabis as opposed to tobacco.

Most of the problems we come across in relation to cannabis use are in relation to mental health issues, and I would say in the period of time I have been a general practitioner, I have seen perhaps three patients whose mental illness is directly related to their cannabis use. One patient had developed a chronic and severe psychotic illness which was thought to be precipitated by his cannabis use, and in two other patients it had precipitated quite a marked depressive illness. It is fairly common to discuss drug use with patients with mental illness, and find that they do have a social use for cannabis, but whether this is a trigger for their mental illness is difficult to say. Beyond those patients I would consider to be seriously and enduringly mentally ill, I would say there is a group of patients on the borders of mental illness who abuse or who use cannabis recreationally, and I quite frequently find that these patients are using cannabis on a daily basis.

Normally they are working and holding down reasonable jobs, often in unskilled trades, and find they use cannabis in the evenings to help them relax when they get home from work.

He concluded by saying: 'It is clear that regular cannabis use often leads to a sense of social detachment and some paranoia amongst these patients and it is not unusual for regular users to feel isolated and present with slightly odd sets of beliefs about their own health.'

To conclude this chapter, the interested reader will find details of further recent studies investigating the links between cannabis use and mental health at the following website: www.schizophrenia.com/prevention/streetdrugs.html (accessed 11 June 2008).

Notes

1   Kirkup, J. and Edwards, R. (2008) *Abuse of cannabis puts 500 a week in hospital, Daily Telegraph,* 11 January.

2   The Royal College of Psychiatrists (2004) 'Schizophrenia: information sheet'. London: The Royal College of Psychiatrists.

3   The Royal College of Psychiatrists (2008) "Depression: information sheet.' London: The Royal College of Psychiatrists.

4   Owen, J. and Mesure, S. (2007) *The great cannabis debate: 50 top experts confirm mental health risk, Independent on Sunday,* UK, 29 July.

Chapter Four

Problem Cannabis Use

In Chapter 3 we discussed the research evidence describing the significant association between cannabis use and episodes of mental illness. Clearly this is one area where cannabis use can become very problematic for the user. However, it is not the only way in which problems can occur. It seems to us that, even if a cannabis user suffers no ill effects on their mental health, there are other ways in which their cannabis use can seriously and negatively affect their lives and well-being.

Over the years, we have had dealings with many hundreds of cannabis users, both young and old, occasional, heavy and habitual users. It has been apparent to us that the vast majority of those users did not see their cannabis use as being a problem to them, although some would admit that their chosen drug caused them to be a little paranoid on occasion, but little else. Indeed, many of them were also users of a wide spectrum of illegal drugs and claimed that whilst one or other of their other drugs caused them problems the cannabis did not. At the same time, it has also been apparent to us that a number of users seemed to have developed such a pattern or intensity of cannabis use that it was beginning to seriously and adversely affect the quality of their lives. Perhaps anecdotes would help to illustrate this. About eight years ago we were contacted by a teacher from a private secondary school in a nearby city in the UK. The teacher requested that we see a former pupil of his who believed he had got himself into real difficulties with cannabis, and wanted help. A meeting was arranged, and the young man, sitting with his girlfriend at his side, told us that he was about to start his second year at university. His fresher year had not gone well despite starting with high hopes, and with an excellent academic record behind him. He had moved into the university's halls of residence and had soon got in with a group of other fresher students who smoked cannabis regularly. He was attracted by their company and soon began to use the drug on a regular basis. This use soon escalated to a daily basis and then several times a day, including what he called a 'wake-up joint' smoked in bed before getting up in the morning. As a result his academic work fell to pieces and he began to miss lectures and to fail to hand in required assignments.

Knowledge of the cannabis use within his hall of residence reached the university authorities and, after trying and failing to deal with it internally, they informed the police. The hall was raided early one morning and this young man was arrested along with several of his friends, resulting in them all receiving an official police caution for cannabis possession. He then received a formal letter from his university warning him that should he become involved with the police again over drug use, or should his attendance at lectures and submission of work not dramatically improve, then he would be dismissed from the university.

The young man went on to tell us that before the police raid he had already made arrangements with his friends from the hall to move into a rented house together for their second year, and indeed had already paid a substantial cash deposit towards the house rental. He had been thinking about his cannabis use over the summer break and had talked it over with his girlfriend. He had come to the conclusion that, directly as a result of his use of the drug, his university degree was in serious danger of going down the drain. He could see what effect that would have on his prospects for the career he desired. With the support of his girlfriend, he had stopped using cannabis over the summer but was afraid that going to live with his friends in the rented student house would place him in great danger of a return to cannabis use with the consequences which that might bring.

Another incident is also worthy of relating. A talented 15-year-old soccer player had been talent spotted whilst playing for his local team by a scout from a leading professional football club. He was invited to attend a trial at the club and whilst impressing the club with his talents was unable, due to his young age, to become a part of their frontline team. However, they offered him regular cash inducements to train with their youth team with a view to him developing his talents further and eventually playing professionally. Unfortunately this small regular income made him popular with his friends back home, many of whom smoked cannabis. He got into using cannabis himself and buying it for his friends, as he was the one who could afford it. The negative aspects of cannabis use quickly took hold and he began to miss soccer training sessions, and to display a 'couldn't care less attitude' which also adversely affected his school work.

After several warnings from the football club and the school, and undergoing counselling in which we were involved, he failed to sufficiently address the problem of his cannabis use, which was causing his amotivational behaviour. As a consequence he failed his school exams and was dropped by the football club, thereby throwing away a potentially very lucrative career.

The experiences of these young people clearly illustrate the types of problem that can arise out of cannabis use.

In this chapter we will try, by reviewing the available evidence, to assess the potential of cannabis use to become seriously problematic. Before doing so it is necessary to decide what we mean by 'problem use'. We intend therefore to take that as meaning any potential for cannabis to be a gateway drug that leads on to other, more serious, drug use, and any potential for cannabis users to become dependent upon the drug.

Is cannabis a gateway drug?

A number of studies[1] have identified three basic truths.

1.   That the use of the so-called harder illegal drugs is typically preceded in the user's 'drug use career' by cannabis (the *order effect*).

2.   The earlier that cannabis is used, the more likely it will be that a person will later use other harder illegal drugs (the *early start effect*).

3.   The higher the frequency of early cannabis use, the more likely it will be that a person will later use other harder illegal drugs (the *higher frequency effect*).

These three straightforward truths are clear enough from the research evidence, and have led to the proposal that cannabis acts as a gateway to later hard drug use: that it in some way predisposes a person to move on to use other drugs, the *causal relationship explanation*.

However, this type of research needs to be carefully examined and understood, because an alternative possible explanation of this apparent relationship between cannabis use and other drug use can also be proposed,[2] namely the *common factor explanation*, which we shall turn to first.

Common factor explanation

The common factor explanation proposes that some factor or group of factors, either genetic or environmental, within or surrounding the user, gives them a propensity to use drugs of one sort or another. In other words, a person may have inherited a genetic predisposition to become drug using from one or both of their parents. Certainly the evidence[3] suggests strongly that such a predisposition can be passed from one generation to the next. It can also be argued strongly that living in very difficult circumstances can lead a person to seek some form of escape through the use of mind-altering drugs. In our work over many years with drug and/or alcohol users, it has been noteworthy how many of them have had very difficult life stories behind them. In the same way, living in an area where drug use is commonplace, and where the whole range of illegal drugs is easily and cheaply available on the streets, can make it much more difficult for a young person to resist drug use themselves.

If we accept the common factor model, then the existence of such a propensity, however it arises, has the power to render a person more likely to use drugs. This model provides a persuasive answer to the three findings detailed earlier of the association between cannabis use and other drug use,

The difference in availability and price between cannabis and other more costly illegal drugs means that it is highly likely that its use will precede other drug use; indeed, the use of cannabis itself will almost always be preceded by alcohol and tobacco use. The order effect is thus simply explained by the normal way in which any human activity progresses, starting at the lowest end and working upwards. Indeed, in all our experience in this field, we can only think of one heroin user with whom we have worked who did not begin their drug career with cannabis.

It also seems a reasonable deduction to propose that those who start cannabis use early, and those who have a high usage of the drug, are more likely to have a stronger propensity to use drugs, as compared with those who start later and use less. If that is so, it seems reasonable to suggest that there is a strong likelihood that such a strengthened propensity will make them more likely to progress their drug use through the lower-level drugs, on to those closer to the top end of the drugs spectrum, providing a reasonable explanation of both the early start and higher frequency effects.

In a study using US survey data of young peoples' drug use,[4] researchers examined the role of cannabis as a precursor of other drug use through the use of a sophisticated mathematical model of the data. They came to the conclusion that a propensity to drug use, however that arises, is a far stronger and more comprehensive explanation of the order, early start and higher frequency effects than any other.

Causal relationship explanation

The causal relationship explanation proposes that there is something intrinsic in cannabis use that predisposes the user to move on to other more serious drugs. The evidence that we will briefly review here suggests that, whilst cannabis use *per se* does not act to predispose the user to further drug use, the act of using *any* pleasure-giving drug regularly *can* act to encourage the user to try other drugs.

Cannabinoids such as THC, along with most of the drugs of misuse such as alcohol, nicotine, opiates and cocaine, have been shown to act on the system of brain structures known as the *reward pathway*.[5] The reward pathway consists of a number of structures within the human brain that are all connected together by a neural pathway called the *medial forebrain bundle*. These structures are involved in the release of neurotransmitters, particularly dopamine, which results in pleasurable feelings of well-being. The reward pathway evolved as a survival aid; thus, eating food, being in a warm sheltered place and having sex all lead to a release of dopamine from parts of the reward pathway. This encourages us to carry on doing these things and thus helps to ensure species survival. Cannabis use acts upon receptors within the nucleus accumbens part of the reward pathway to instigate the release of dopamine, and thus the same feelings of well-being.

The stimulation of the reward pathway by drug use can lead to very intense feelings of well-being and pleasure, and lead to it being commandeered by drug use so that other dopamine-producing behaviours become less important. This commandeering has the potential to lead to the user trying other, stronger drugs and, perhaps more importantly, those with a more immediate action,[6] to achieve even higher and more immediate releases of dopamine. So perhaps the causal relationship explanation has some truth in it: use of cannabis can lead to other drug use. However, we still need to ask the question, 'Is there something special about cannabis that causes this?'

What the research seems to have established is that repeated use of *any* drug, not just cannabis, that stimulates the reward pathway can lead to use of another. Also apparent is the tendency to move to those drugs that produce more immediate effects. It is the so-called harder drugs such as cocaine, amphetamine and the opiates which produce the quickest effects.[7] As previously discussed, due to its relatively low price and easy availability, cannabis is likely to appear early on in a person's drug-using career, as will nicotine and alcohol, which also appeared in the list of drugs acting on the reward pathway. This gives the appearance that cannabis, along with nicotine and alcohol, has acted as a specific gateway to other drug use. In our view the evidence suggests that it is the act of regular drug use that leads to other, more serious drug use, and not the use of cannabis or any other single drug *per se*.

So let us sum this up and answer the question, 'Can cannabis act as a gateway drug?' with the clear answer, 'Yes'. However, that answer can also be given for other drugs as well, for the evidence suggests very strongly that the regular use of any pleasure-giving drug, perhaps instigated by the propensity to use discussed earlier, can act as a gateway to other more serious drug use. We are reminded of an alcoholic with whom we once worked, who once said that he found it 'easier to leave the cork in the bottle than to replace it once he had taken it out'. Perhaps the same conclusion can be drawn from the evidence presented in this chapter. It seems that once a person 'takes the cork out' and begins to use mind-altering drugs of any type then they run the risk that they may not be able to 'put the cork back in', and may progress further along the drug road than they intended.

Cannabis dependency

The question as to whether a user can become addicted to cannabis arouses very strong emotions in a lot of people. Many cannabis user websites dismiss any suggestion of an addiction potential in cannabis as simply being a myth created by authority to justify its present legal position. The Cannabis Campaign Guide[8] organization describes on its website the question of cannabis addiction thus: 'It is very clear that it is a mere Prohibitionist's ploy, a rank deception, to introduce "Psychological dependence" as a "criterion" for prohibition regulations because the only non-addictive substance to which prohibition apply [sic] is...cannabis.' The US website Drug WarRant[9] says '[the evidence] fairly effectively debunks the myth of marijuana as an addictive drug. This is something that is common sense to those who are familiar with how marijuana works, but it's an important refutation to the drug warriors' claims.' The US Drug Policy Alliance[10] website is a little more restrained: 'Marijuana does not cause physical dependence. If people experience withdrawal symptoms at all, they are remarkably mild.' Interestingly the Cannabis Campaign Guide website quotes from the 1929 Panama Canal Zone military investigations into cannabis use, by Panama canal building workers, in support of its view: 'there is no evidence that Marihuana as grown and used [in the Canal Zone] is a "habit-forming" drug.' In our search for truth and understanding perhaps we need to look at some scientific evidence on the subject that is less than 80 years old.

So what is the evidence? Is cannabis an addictive drug in the sense that its use has the potential to lead to a true physical or psychological dependence upon its further use? Until recently, the accepted wisdom has been that cannabis does not lead to any form of physical dependency. This can no longer be claimed, as a growing body of scientific evidence begins to demonstrate the existence of a clear cannabis withdrawal syndrome.[11] Such a syndrome demonstrates that the use of cannabis has led to an alteration in bodily function which in turn leads to a series of clinically significant symptoms, if cannabis is withdrawn.[12] What also appears clear is that the heavier the use of cannabis, and the longer its duration, the more likely it is that the withdrawal symptoms will be more severe should cannabis use be discontinued. However, it is very important to say that, for the vast majority of cannabis users who cease to use the drug, the withdrawal symptoms that they experience will be mild and within most people's ability to handle. These symptoms may include restlessness, irritability, agitation, anxiety, depression, loss of appetite, insomnia and sleep disturbance due to strange dreams, nausea, cramping, and craving for continued use of cannabis. This is a fairly impressive list, and experienced, usually in a mild form lasting from between two and ten days, by around 50 per cent of discontinuing cannabis users. One research study[13] in this field likens the cannabis withdrawal syndrome in type and magnitude to that experienced by those giving up smoking tobacco cigarettes. Most cigarette smokers who give up their habit would probably agree that the withdrawal symptoms they suffered were difficult but within their ability to handle. Some tobacco cigarette smokers, however, particularly those with a heavy or long-established habit, have great difficulty in giving up cigarettes, and need to seek pharmaceutical help in the form of nicotine substitution therapy, such as transdermal nicotine patches or gum. Some may need further help in the form of counselling, acupuncture or hypnotherapy. So it is with some cannabis users who wish to give up their habit. They find it beyond their ability through will alone, and need the assistance of various forms of recovery therapy, including pharmaceutical therapy, counselling, group and family therapy, cognitive behavioural therapy, life direction guidance and hypnotherapy.

Strong evidence of such a need for help is provided by the multitude of organizations currently offering treatment for 'cannabis addiction'. Many of these organizations[14] offer 'self-assessment' online tests through their websites, which allow users who suspect that they may have a problem with their cannabis use to gauge the level of their dependency. The majority of the self-assessment tests that we have seen all appear to be identical, and take the form of the same 12 questions. We are unable to find out who originated the test, but it is fairly short and worth repeating here verbatim.

1. Has smoking cannabis stopped being fun?

2. Do you plan your life around your smoking cannabis?

3. Do you ever get high by yourself?

4. When your cannabis supply is almost gone, are you worried about how to get more?

5. Do you smoke cannabis to help you deal with your feelings?

6. Is it hard for you to think about your life without cannabis?

7. Do you find that you choose your friends based on your cannabis use?

8. Do you smoke cannabis to avoid facing your problems?

9. Has your use of cannabis caused problems with your memory, concentration or motivation?

10. Does your cannabis use let you live in a privately defined world?

11. Have you ever not kept promises you made to yourself to cut down or control your cannabis smoking?

12. Have your friends or relatives ever complained that your cannabis smoking is causing problems with your relationship with them?

The person taking the test is advised that if they answer 'yes' to any of the questions they may have a dependency problem with cannabis. Clearly the more 'yes' answers that are given then the more likely it is that the person taking is test is developing a dependency on the drug.

A number of the questions used in this self-assessment test relate to the psychological relationship between the user and their drug. Questions 5, 6, 8 and 10 are clearly of this type, and provide a window directly into how the user feels psychologically about their cannabis use. This raises the issue of a psychological dependence on cannabis as distinct from a purely physical type. Questions 6, 8, and 10 all question the user as to whether they are using cannabis as a form of escape from the less than desirable realities of their lives, whilst question 6 is highly relevant, asking the user how they would feel about life without cannabis. In the course of our work, we have met and worked with many cannabis users who felt strongly that they would not be able to cope with their lives without their drug. All of this is touching upon how the user feels psychologically about the role of cannabis in their lives, and how they would cope with life without it. It seems self-evident to us that whether a person is developing a physical dependency which may lead to withdrawal symptoms should use be discontinued, or whether their problems in giving up are wholly psychological, makes no difference. They simply have a habit that will be difficult for them to break.

One more point is worth making on this topic. The existence of so many 'cannabis addiction treatment organizations' provides direct evidence of the large numbers of cannabis users who are finding difficulty in giving up their drug, and seeking outside help. Many of these organizations are non-profit making, whilst others are run on a commercial profit-making basis, but none would exist unless there was a need for them to service. Whatever the strength of the research evidence pointing to the existence of a distinct cannabis withdrawal syndrome, the clear fact is that many users of the drug find that they have great difficulty in giving it up without a great deal of professional help.

Notes

1   Fergusson, D.M. and Horwood, L.J. (2000) 'Does cannabis use encourage other forms of illicit drug use?' *Addiction 95*, 505–20; Fergusson, D.M., Boden, J.M. and Horwood, L.J. (2006) 'Cannabis use and other illicit drug use: testing cannabis gateway hypothesis.' *Addiction 101*, 40, 556–69; Kandel, D.B. and Yamaguchi, K. (1993) 'From beer to crack: developmental patterns of drug involvement.' *American Journal of Public Health 85*, 851–3;

2   Hall, W. and Lynskey, M. (2005) 'Is cannabis a gateway drug? Testing hypotheses about the relationship between cannabis use and the use of other illicit drugs.' *Drug and Alcohol Review 24*, 1, 39–48.

3   van den Bree, M., Svikis, D. and Pickens, R. (1998) 'Genetic influences in antisocial personality and drug use disorders.' *Drug and Alcohol Dependence 49*, 3, 177–87.

4   Morral, A.R., McCaffrey, D.F. and Paddock, S.M. (2002) 'Reassessing the marijuana gateway effect.' *Addiction 97*, 1492–504.

5   Gardner, E.L. (2002) 'Addictive potential of cannabinoids: The underlying neurobiology.' *Chemistry and Physics of Lipids 12*, 267–90; Mechoulam, R. and Parker, L. (2003) 'Cannabis and alcohol: A close friendship.' *Trends in Pharmacological Sciences 24*, 266–8.

6   Carlson, N.R. (2004) *Physiology of Behavior.* London: Allyn and Bacon.

7   Julien, R.M. (2005) *A Primer of Drug Action.* New York: Worth Publishers.

8   Cannabis Campain Guide 'Canabis addiction and cannabis dependency – a myth?' (available at www.ccguide.org.uk/psychological-dependence.php, accessed February 2008).

9   Drug WarRant (2004) 'Marijuana shown not addictive, not gateway'. 9 May (available at http://blogs.salon.com/0002762/2004/05/09.html, accessed February 2008).

10   Drug Policy Alliance Network 'Myths and and facts about marijuana.' (available at www.drugpolicy.org/marijuana/factsmyths/, accessed February 2008).

11   Julien, R.M. (2005) *A Primer of Drug Action.* New York: Worth Publishers.

12   Lichtman, A. and Martin, B. (2002) 'Marijuana withdrawal syndrome in the animal model.' *Journal of Clinical Pharmacology 42*, 11, S20–S27; Smith, N. (2002) 'A review of the published literature in cannabis withdrawal symptoms in human users.' *Addiction 97*, 621–32.

13   Budney, A., Hughes, J., Moore, B. and Novy, P. (2001) 'Marijuana abstinence effects in marijuana smokers maintained in their home environment.' *Archive of General Psychiatry 58*, 917–24.

14   For example, Marijuana Anonymous World Services, Van Nuys, CA; Choose Help Addiction Treatment Centers, Long Beach, CA.

Chapter Five

Treatment Options

The issue of whether or not cannabis users can develop a dependency on the drug is discussed in Chapter 4. That chapter makes the point that there are a very large number of organizations offering cannabis addiction recovery services. In this chapter we will discuss the different type of services on offer, and the various techniques that they utilize.

For many people, their use of cannabis may not, in their eyes at least, constitute a problem. They may think that they are only using the drug recreationally, to be sociable, for spiritual enrichment or for relaxation, and are easily able to afford what they use. They may think that they are not suffering from any psychological or physical problems as a result of their use, and that they are not in any real danger of doing so. Indeed, they may appear to have the entire situation under control, and for many of them it can remain this way. Certainly the majority of users start out like this; after all, no one begins using cannabis with the expectation that they will develop a problem with it. But situations have an unfortunate way of changing for the worst over time, and for many it may turn out to be quite a different story.

Cannabis use for some may have reached a point where it is adversely affecting their physical and mental health, their finances, employment, relationships, education, their legal position and even accommodation. Many users, despite clear evidence to the contrary, will still choose not to see their cannabis use as a problem, and may simply transfer any problem back onto others who may be affected, or who are showing concern, insisting that they are making something out of nothing. Eventually, however, some cannabis users may reach a point where, despite their wish to ignore the facts, there is no alternative but to admit to having a problem for which they may require help, support and understanding.

Depending on the degree and length of time of their cannabis usage, whether they use any other drugs, the existence of any physical or mental health illness, and any other life problems faced by the user, there will be a range of services available to them, and to others connected with them, who are affected in some way. But, however good these services are, they can only succeed in helping if the user is fully willing to co-operate and be totally honest with themselves and others.

Local drug services

Many large towns and cities will have drug and substance misuse services located in them. These may be statutory or voluntary in nature, will be staffed or supported by trained personnel, and offer a range of services to users and others alike. Many have trained counsellors, therapists and medical staff, any of whom may be assigned as key worker to the user, after an initial assessment interview to determine their needs. Counselling may be offered on a one-to-one basis or in groups and, in some cases, proves to be all that is needed to overcome the user's problems and help them to become cannabis-free.

Relapse prevention counselling may then follow to ensure that they remain cannabis-free. Some agencies may offer alternatives to counselling, such as life direction coaching, hypnotherapy, acupuncture, stress management and relaxation classes, or even sport and exercise sessions.

Detoxification

No substitute drug is currently available to assist users in weaning themselves off cannabis in the way that, for example, methadone is used to assist heroin users to discontinue use of their drug. However, some limited help is available in the form of prescribed medicines to assist those cannabis users who experience real difficulty in coping with their withdrawal symptoms.

A small number of pharmaceutical drugs have been the subject of trials with cannabis users attempting to give up their drug use. A study involving the use of Nefazodone,[1] an anti-depressant drug marketed under the trade name Serzone™, found that, whilst some beneficial effect was seen in alleviating anxiety and muscle pain felt by a number of cannabis users during withdrawal, no effect was seen on participants' ratings of irritability, poor sleep quality and feelings of being miserable. In a pilot study,[2] the anti-anxiety drug Buspirone achieved a 50 per cent reduction in use of cannabis as compared with a control group. A study[3] involving the use of the anti-depressant drug Fluoxetine with participants who were dependent upon both alcohol and cannabis, and who exhibited symptoms of depression and suicidal tendencies, also showed robust beneficial effects on their use of cannabis. Although these studies do show some promise of a suitable pharmacotherapy for withdrawing cannabis users, a great deal of research remains to be done.

Despite the limited degree of supporting medication, a large number of cannabis addiction recovery centres offer various forms of detoxification for both inpatients and outpatients. The detoxification process, of clearing cannabis from the user's system and allowing the body to adjust accordingly, may be achieved reasonably quickly, bearing in mind the long half-life of cannabis, especially if the user is fully committed to becoming 'clean'. This commitment may be due to the influence of other people, the desire to remain in a job, for travel or legal purposes, or even because of pregnancy or illness. The process, however, may take much longer for others and may never be totally achieved at all.

Detoxification can take place at home if necessary, especially where support is given by the user's family and friends, or where a residential programme would be impracticable, as in the case of a parent who is unable to leave their children. Many cannabis addiction recovery services will support this kind of venture, making frequent home visits to the user and enabling them to remain in the familiarity and safety of their own surroundings.

Other services will require the user to enter outpatient day detoxification clinics or specialized residential detoxification units, sometimes located within psychiatric hospitals, for which they may first need a referral by their doctor.

If committed to prison, some users will have to detox against their will, and the regime may be unsympathetic, with the reducing period being rather short and painful with little back-up or support. Happily this situation is becoming less common, as many prisons are now changing for the better with regard to making their new inmates drug- and substance-free, with drug-free wings and dedicated substance misuse workers.

If they are to work well, detoxification programmes have to be carefully planned. The pros and cons need to be discussed at length and questions such as 'Why now?', 'Is this the best time?', 'Have I enough support services?' and 'What happens afterwards?' will have to be addressed. If, during this process, some of the user's other life problems, which may well have led to their cannabis misuse in the first place, are not dealt with, then they may simply be setting themselves up to fail. Such a failure will inevitably lead to the user going straight back to their usual way of coping, by re-using cannabis or other substances.

Similarly, large lifestyle changes may have to be considered. Changing one's circle of friends or even moving house may be thought of as necessary by some, in order to keep clear of familiar people, places and circumstances, any of which may trigger off thoughts of former drug use and lead again to a new bout of craving. It is therefore clear that detoxification is best carried out with professional and medical help in order for it to have a chance of success, although some brave souls have managed it on their own.

Rehabs

Residential rehabilitation facilities, known as 'rehabs', exist for users who seriously want to get away from substance misuse of all kinds, including cannabis, and get their lives back together. But this option is time consuming, can be expensive and is in great demand. There are four main types of rehabs, each with their own regime or working methods.

The first that we shall consider is the 'general rehab' which acts rather like a small community. Its residents may well be able to decide on their own communal needs and rules, and counselling is carried out both individually and in group sessions. The average length of stay in this type of establishment is between six and eight months.

The second type of rehab is the Christian-based establishment which normally offers one-to-one counselling only, rather than group work. Residents here may be expected to adopt a Christian outlook in order to help them overcome their drug problems. This may involve regular Bible study groups, prayer sessions and religious services and may therefore be unacceptable to some users. The average length of stay in such establishments may be anything up to a year.

The third type of rehab, known as 'concept rehabs', is a highly structured establishments where the resident's time is filled to capacity. Therapeutic sessions here are both intense and somewhat confrontational, allowing users to get in touch with and express their feelings openly. Users' self-image and lifestyle may also be broken down systematically in order to then rebuild them in a more acceptable way. As this way of working can prove to be too much for some residents, the drop-out rate can be quite high, wasting precious resources. Average length of stay, for those who last the course, is between 9 and 18 months.

The last type of rehab utilizes something called the 'Minnesota Method', a programme based on the 12 steps to sobriety used by Alcoholics Anonymous. Substance misuse is considered by advocates of the Minnesota method to be a lifelong illness that requires constant counselling to avoid relapse. Residents' days here are very long and organized, with an individual's progress measured and assessed by both peers and rehab workers alike. The average length of stay at this type of establishment is quite short, being perhaps only between six and eight weeks. However, 'halfway houses' run by the rehab may then offer ongoing placement to former rehab residents, for anything up to a further 12 months. During this time they are offered further support before being totally integrated back into everyday society, where they must then fend for themselves.

Rehab is not for the faint hearted, and the different regimes must be studied carefully before the correct choice can be made. As residential establishments, they may well be situated far from the user's familiar haunts. This may be considered as an advantage by some who may want to get away from their previous lives. Others, however, may not wish to be so far from home due to commitments such as children, family or friends whom they do not wish to leave too far behind.

A number of charitable organizations offer low-cost residential rehabilitation services for cannabis users, but demand generally outstrips the supply of available places. In some cases, dependent upon their financial circumstances or that of their families, users could be asked to contribute towards the costs of their treatment.

Before being accepted to any rehab, all potential residents will first be assessed as to their suitability, and then interviewed to ensure that they have the right level of commitment. Similarly, it will be decided whether the particular rehab can meet their needs. These procedures, together with the issue of securing adequate funding, mean that there may be a delay between the user deciding to go to a rehab and their actually being admitted.

There are fewer rehabs catering specifically for women than there are for men, possibly reflecting the greater use of drug and other substances by men than by women, although this difference is narrowing in many countries. Generally, there are even fewer establishments that can cater for those with mental health problems, pregnant women, or women with dependent children.

Last, it is worth stating that residential rehabilitation may not always be completely successful. This may be because of many factors, not least the determination and co-operation of the user, and the degree of support available to them once they leave. Some may have to make several rehab attempts before they can say that they have totally conquered their drug habits, and have dealt fully with the reasons that led to them being there in the first instance.

Home detoxification/rehabilitation

A number of cannabis recovery organizations offer home-based detoxification and rehabilitation treatment. This has the obvious advantage that it allows the client to remain in their own surroundings during the treatment, which may alleviate some problems connected with child care and other responsibilities, and may also be cheaper, but has the major disadvantage of allowing the client to remain within the social context surrounding their cannabis usage. The amount of support available to the client varies from one organization to the next. Some organizations will even arrange for a member of staff to 'live in' with the client during the important first few days or weeks, whilst other organizations offer much less one to one support, or only a rather impersonal 'correspondence course' type methodology.

Self-help

Certain web-based organizations, drug services, doctors surgeries or helplines may be able to supply publications giving details on how to reduce or discontinue cannabis use on request (see Appendix 2 for a list of sources of self-help information and advice).

It is impossible in a short chapter such as this to detail all of the ways in which a cannabis user who is having difficulty in giving up such use can receive the help necessary for them to successfully become cannabis-free. For details of all the available services in each locality, a simple search of the telephone directory or a search of the Internet may reveal the information required. Details of local services may also be available from local doctors and hospitals, pharmacists, the police, social services and citizens' advice bureaux (see Appendix 3 for a list of rehabilitation organizations).

Notes

1   Haney, M., Hart, C., Ward, A. and Foltin, R. (2003) 'Nefazodone decreases anxiety during marijuana withdrawal in human.' *Psychopharmacology 165*, 157–65.

2   McRae, L., Brady, K. and Carter, R. (2006) 'Buspirone for treatment of marijuana dependence: A pilot study.' *American Journal on Addictions 15*, 404.

3   Cornelius, J., Salloum, I., Lynch, K., Clark, D. and Mann, J. (2001) 'Treating the substance-abusing suicidal patient.' *Annals of the New York Academy of Sciences 932*, 78–93.

Chapter Six

Detecting Cannabis Use

Testing for the presence of cannabis use in an individual is nowadays, due to the sophisticated technology currently available, a very simple affair that does not even require the skills of a medical professional to read the result.

The most commonly used screening tests are those that use samples of urine or saliva, which can be carried out almost anywhere, without the need for laboratory facilities. They are relatively cheap, and give an almost instant visible result with, in some systems, a readable printout.

Another test favoured by some is carried out on human hair from any part of the body which, dependent upon its length, can give a historical perspective on the drug usage of its owner for up to two years! This type of test, however, requires laboratory facilities, and is consequently much more expensive.

The drawback with each of these methods is that they are unable to provide quantitative results, so that the degree of use cannot be readily determined. Of course, no test can determine what was in the user's mind when the drug was taken, whether the use was active or passive, or whether, indeed, the drug was administered to the person without their knowledge. Similarly, these tests cannot show whether the user is currently under the influence of the drug, only that they have used it within a specific time frame. This is especially difficult with cannabis as, due to the nature of the drug, its metabolites tend to be excreted much more slowly from the body than do those for cocaine or heroin, for example. So a positive result for cannabis could show usage that is days or even weeks old. But even this could be used to advantage by those requiring the test, where the object of the exercise is to prohibit use totally, and therefore detect where this has been infringed.

Testing is carried out for a wide range of purposes and by a variety of agencies and individuals to determine the usage of cannabis or other drugs. These agencies include:

- medical services

- the police

- schools and colleges

- employers

- the military

- the courts, probation service and prisons

- social services

- parents, guardians and partners

- concerned or worried users.

But, before testing takes place, much consideration must be given by those requesting or carrying out the testing as to what the results will actually show, and what the repercussions will be of a positive or negative result. Let us now consider why certain agencies may test specifically for cannabis.

Medical services

Testing for medical reasons is sometimes carried out in psychiatric units to check whether newly admitted or current patients have been using cannabis. Psychiatrists have known for many years that cannabis can precipitate some psychotic symptoms,[1] or exacerbate existing ones in those with a mental health disorder. Testing can aid in diagnosis and treatment, and could alert the medical authorities to illicit substance use by inpatients already in treatment. It may also be of benefit to doctors where cannabis use is contra-indicated with the prescribing of other medications for certain conditions.

Some medical drug services will also screen for cannabis to ensure that patients who have subscribed to an abstinence-based programme are adhering to the rules.

Similarly, some drug services may provide screening for cannabis on request, so that a negative result could be shown to an employer, partner, probation officer etc., or a positive result could warn the user that they could potentially 'get caught out' by another test due to be held in the near future.

The police

Primarily, the police will test for cannabis (and other substances) to help determine whether somebody is fit to drive, for example, and nowadays this can even be carried out at the roadside. But, as these tests cannot determine exactly when the drug was used, the user's degree of impairment and what amount of cannabis was used, it will need to be accompanied by a standard impairment test, which will include examination of pupil size, walking, balance, co-ordination, perception of time and spatial awareness. Police can, in certain circumstances, also request that a blood sample be taken for later, more detailed, analysis.

Users of cannabis will be aware that taking the drug can alter their perception of distance and time, reduce their powers of concentration and co-ordination, narrow their field of vision and slow their reaction times, but this may not become apparent to them when driving until they are faced with an unexpected situation.

So the best solution is, as with alcohol, not to drive at all if you have recently used cannabis and may still be affected; for potentially you will put your driving licence at risk, not to mention your life and the lives of others. You may also face fines or even a prison sentence.

In some Australian states, when a driver is stopped, a preliminary saliva test is taken, and if found to be positive a confirmatory second saliva test is carried out. If found to be positive once again, the sample is sent off to a laboratory for gas chromatography mass spectrometry testing. If this laboratory sample again proves positive, then a prosecution could follow.

Many other countries across the world are introducing similar roadside testing procedures.

Educational establishments

Many schools and colleges nowadays trade on their academic results, especially the independent residential fee-paying kind that almost guarantee good grade passes. All schools and colleges have the duty of acting *in loco parentis* for their charges, making them responsible for the children's health and welfare. This applies particularly to residential establishments.

With the knowledge that cannabis use can adversely affect concentration, memory and motivation, many schools in Britain have introduced mandatory drug testing[2] to encourage the best possible outcomes academically, and to reduce any physical or psychological harm due to the use of illegal substances by students.

Many of the best-known private schools routinely drug screen some or all of their students, and penalties for use can be most severe, resulting in expulsions or even police involvement. Usually, testing is put in place due to 'information received' or 'evidence found', but can also be introduced due to the school's observation of changed or uncharacteristic behaviour in a pupil, or unexpected underachievement in suspicious circumstances.

Some British state schools have also been given governmental approval to conduct random drug screening of students, as is commonplace already within the US, and, if carried out, this could bring the benefits of early identification and intervention intended to prevent an escalation of the problem in individuals or groups. Random drug screening can also have a deterrent effect on some, whilst affording others a credible reason to say no to offers of cannabis by their peers.

Drug screening in schools is more often than not of the non-invasive saliva-testing variety, allowing those being tested to keep their dignity, rather than having to be observed whilst producing a urine sample. Saliva testing also affords less chance of being falsified than urine samples, which can be contaminated with the addition of adulterants or be substituted with urine from another source (especially if not observed). The subject can also make the excuse that they just cannot produce a urine sample on demand.

All educational establishments should have a comprehensive drugs policy, so that no one is left in any doubt as to the stance taken on illicit drug use and testing, the consequences that may flow from a positive test and also the measures that will be put in place to safeguard privacy and confidentially.

Once tested, if a saliva or urine sample proves positive, further, more detailed laboratory-testing procedures may be considered, to eliminate the diminishing possibility, due to ever more sophisticated technology, of a false positive result.

All educational establishments should also ensure that drugs awareness sessions are available to students and staff, and that those who wish to seek help and advice regarding a substance misuse problem have the opportunity to do so.

Drug screening at work

Because of the deleterious effects of cannabis use and its slow excretion time from the body, use of the drug by employees could also adversely affect colleagues and co-workers, as well as affect the overall operation, safety and efficiency of their place of work.

As with educational establishments, employers should have in place a drugs policy which clearly explains to the current workforce, prospective employees and contractors just what is expected of them regarding the use of substances whilst at work or being under their influence. This is especially so for those professions or areas of employment where safety is paramount, such as the transport and construction industries.

Awareness and implementation of such a policy is beneficial for all concerned, as it could:

- reduce absenteeism

- improve productivity

- reduce accidents

- enhance company reputation and reassure customers

- allow those with concerns or a problem to seek early help, and be dealt with supportively and compassionately.

In many countries employers have a legal responsibility to ensure that, as far as possible, the health, welfare and safety of their workforce and any visitors to their work sites are assured, taking all practical steps to carry this out. This responsibility may include the prevention of illegal substance misuse on their premises, including company transport. If an employer knowingly allows an employee at work to use drugs or be under the influence of such a substance, then they themselves may be liable to prosecution.

As employees may not volunteer the information that they misuse illegal substances (or legal, in the case of alcohol, prescription drugs, or even solvents) whilst at work, or are still under the influence whilst carrying out their duties, good employers will need to be aware of several indicators that could potentially be linked to such use. These will include:

- the employee's sickness record

- unexplained absenteeism

- long and frequent breaks

- uncharacteristic changes in behaviour

- reduced performance and productivity

- deterioration in colleague relationships.

Investigating indicators of this nature will, of course, have to be handled very sensitively, as the problems noted may not have arisen due to the use of substances, but be as a consequence of other issues in the employee's life, such as difficulties at home or illness.

Drug screening is sometimes performed after a workplace accident or 'near-miss incident' to ensure that no one involved was impaired in any way at the time. This is due to the fact that a positive result could adversely affect the outcome of any insurance or compensation claim made as a result, or have a bearing on any legal proceedings.

The degree of drug use is generally lower amongst those in work, compared with those not in employment, but this gap is diminishing.[3] The degree of use of illicit substances by younger workers may be greater than for older workers due to their social milieux.

One of the main aims of a project report[4] published by the UK Health and Safety Executive in 2004 was to determine the possibility of an association between the use of illegal substances and the degree of reported accidents and incidents at work. The findings showed that:

- There was an impact by drug use on cognitive performance, mirrored by an association with cognitive failures at work.

- There was an association between cannabis usage and work-related road traffic accidents, among those with other risk factors.

- There was an association between substance use and minor injuries among those with other minor injury risk factors in their work.

- The recreational use of substances may adversely affect performance and safety at work.

Overall, however, the project team believed that more extensive research was required to assess further the relationship between workplace accidents and substance use.

The military

Drug testing is well established among many of the armed services around the world, especially in the West, and this is not surprising due to their complex and dangerous roles, and the increasing utilization of sophisticated technology and weaponry.

Despite these measures, however, a report published in December 2007[5] showed that the British Army was losing the equivalent of a battalion a year due to illegal drug use, with almost 800 troops being discharged in 2006 as a result of positive drug tests. Looking specifically at cannabis, figures in the report showed that 288 positive tests were recorded in 2003 and 278 in 2006, demonstrating a slight reduction, whereas positive cocaine tests had escalated more than threefold in the same period, from 126 to 423! A spokesman for the Ministry of Defence stated in response, 'Positive rates in the Army over the past four years average around 0.77%, compared with over 7% in civilian workplace drug testing programmes'.[6]

Compulsory drug screening was first introduced into the British Army in 1998, when the policy was very much zero tolerance based. However, since then this policy has been relaxed, and this is thought to have come about due to re-cruitment difficulties as a consequence of the recent interventions in Iraq and Afghanistan. In 2003 an Early Intervention Programme was introduced whereby junior personnel in all three services who tested positive to drugs had the opportunity to remain in their chosen careers by completing a four-day course consisting of educational workshops, assessments, and group and indi-vidual counselling sessions. Completion of the course does not guarantee that any participant will be able to remain in uniform. Writing in 2006,[7] Major Angela Herbert, the Army's Substance Misuse Staff Officer, stated that 'the course gives the Army the opportunity to gain a better understanding of individ-uals before deciding whether they should be discharged or retained. Partici-pants...must show remorse for what they have done...and pass all the tests.'

The American Department of Defense (DOD) has also taken a zero-tolerance attitude to drug use, and through education and deterrence claimed to have reduced drug use significantly within all areas of the military, including civilian workers. The DOD reports that, back in 1983, around 25 per cent of personnel would have been using illegal drugs, but this had dropped to just 3 per cent by 1998.

Illegal drug use is taken very seriously by the DOD, and the Deputy Assis-tant Secretary of Defense for Counternarcotics, Andre Hollis,[8] has explained that, although the services do not take everyone to court for illegal drug use, most will not be allowed to remain on active duty. Hollis also believes that edu-cating troops on the dangers and consequences of illegal drug use is the duty of all military leaders, and that the impairment of cognitive functions is of particu-lar concern 'where our young people are in charge of, and responsible for so-phisticated pieces of equipment'. An expert on drug testing in Hollis's office, Colonel Mick Smith, concurred with this, stating that: 'Military people have a dangerous job. They operate heavy equipment and use complex integrated computer systems.'

All US active duty service members will undergo a urine drug screen test each year, with reservists being tested biannually. Not all urine samples are tested for all drugs, but they are all tested for cocaine, amphetamines (including ecstasy) and cannabis. The DOD operates six urine-testing laboratories for this purpose, testing 60,000 samples each month. In 2001, 70 per cent of the

16,759 drug users identified through testing were cannabis users,[9] a slight reduction on the figures for the previous year.

Colonel Smith is aware that cannabis is 'not a safe drug' and that it can have 'long term effects on the brain', but that it still remains the most heavily used illegal drug within the US military. Because the stakes are so high nowadays, Colonel Smith stated that 'we don't have time for that [drugs], particularly when we are fighting a war', as it 'interferes with as unit's ability to complete their mission'.[10]

A new US military drugs policy was introduced in 2002,[11] which involved more frequent random testing of active duty personnel, reservists and civilian employees, in order to reduce demand for and the use of illegal drugs within the DOD. Drug use is seen as totally incompatible with military service, and this is made very clear to all potential recruits.

Methods of testing

Let us now look at the most common testing methods to determine the benefits and drawbacks of each.

Urine screening

This type of test is generally thought to give accurate and reliable results and, due to this, is the most likely to stand up to any legal challenge. It has the added advantage of being quick and inexpensive. The 'window of detection' that this test affords is generally up to four or five days for most drugs, but for cannabis may be up to one week for single usage and up to three months for continual heavy use.

Unfortunately, the test is sometimes considered as degrading and embarrassing and, unless the sample is produced 'under observation', there exists the opportunity to add adulterants, substitute with someone else's urine or dilute the sample. Urine samples also need to be treated as potential biological hazards, necessitating specialized handling and forwarding arrangements if sent for laboratory testing.

On the spot 'dip stick' testing strips, or 'cassette' tests, can be used almost anywhere, as long as there are suitable disposal and washing facilities. These types of test actively 'search' for the metabolites of the drug, which are produced by the liver as part of the natural process of breaking down and removing the drug from the bloodstream. They generally consist of an absorbent area where the urine is introduced (usually two to four drops only), which then moves by capillary action to the testing area.

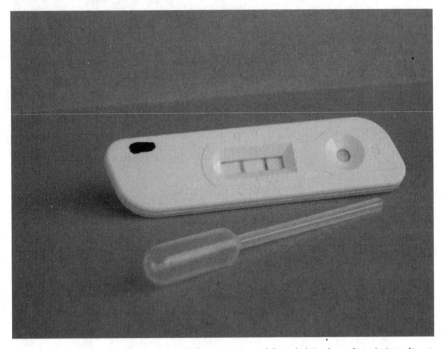

Figure 6.1: Cassette test (with pipette) showing control line (C) and test line (T), indicating a negative result

The control line (C) becomes visible to give assurance that the test is working properly, and the test line (T) will only become visible if the sample is negative or below the amount that could be in the sample due to passive smoking, as the tests are specifically calibrated to filter out the possibility of a positive result due to passive inhaling.

If the sample is positive, the metabolites of the drug in the urine will prevent a preset dye from adhering to the test line, which thus remains non-visible. There are now also available sealable specimen cups that have built-in detection strips, which makes for ease of handling and disposal.

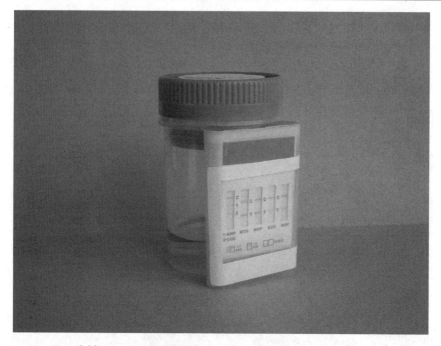

Figure 6.2: Sealable specimen cup with built-in testing strips

Saliva screening (oral fluid)

The greatest benefit of oral fluid screening is that the gathering of the sample can be observed directly, is easily carried out almost anywhere, including at the roadside, and is highly resistant to tampering. The greatest drawback to this type of test is that the detection window is much reduced, down to between 8 and 24 hours. Cannabis and its metabolites are not detectable in saliva for as long as in urine, and this method of testing is known therefore to be less reliable in detecting cannabis use than other methods.

The test is carried out by placing a small absorbent pad, mounted at one end of a hollow tube, in the mouth between the gum and the cheek, where it collects oral fluids. To ensure that enough fluid is collected, some devices have an inbuilt indicator at the opposite end of the tube which protrudes from the mouth, which changes colour when the required amount has been collected. The absorbent pad is then broken off and placed within a small container in which there is a 'carrier' fluid. The pad is then compressed in the container to force the oral fluid into the carrier fluid. The resulting mixture is then collected in a pipette, and a few drops are added to a testing cassette, not unlike that for urine, and the results can be read directly by a trained operative. Alternatively, the cassette may be placed within a portable electronic testing machine which can give both a visual result and, in some cases, a print-out. Oral fluid samples may also be sent for laboratory testing.

Hair testing

This type of screening has the longest 'window of detection' of them all, dependent upon the length of hair being tested. Hair samples can be taken from any part of the body, but most usually from the head. As human hair grows at the rate of about ½ inch (1.3 cm) per month, a specimen 12 inches long could give results for the previous two years! This type of testing cannot, however, detect very recent drug use, as drug metabolites take a few days to be deposited in the hair from the bloodstream. However, it can detect long-term chronic use of a substance.

The collecting of the sample is not invasive, embarrassing or degrading, and the possibility of the donor tampering with it prior to collection is minimized. Hair samples are also more stable than urine or saliva, as they tend not to deteriorate over time, and therefore handling is less problematical. On the downside, this type of test will require laboratory procedures and its current cost therefore makes it less attractive, especially as a means of ongoing screening (rather than a one-off investigation). It is currently used by the police in the UK to screen potential recruits.

The use of drug sniffer dogs

Before we leave the subject of testing, it is worth spending a moment looking at the use of dogs specially trained to 'sniff' for the presence of drugs. Cannabis can be detected due to its characteristic smell, which is caused by *terpenes* contained within the plant. With varieties known as skunk and super-skunk, it does not take a genius to understand that the aroma of raw or even burned cannabis can be quite pungent. The smell will permeate clothing and soft furnishings (rather like tobacco), and in many cases is characterized by its sickly sweet odour which is unmistakable.

Trained dogs, with their acute sense of smell, are ideally suited to the task of sniffing out hidden drugs, and can be seen in daily use at airports, at ports, in police searches and in prisons. The use of sniffer dogs could also be considered for educational establishments.

Notes

1   Royal College of Psychiatrists (2001) 'Cannabis use has adverse effects on mental health.' Press release, 1 February.

2   *Drug Testing, Times Education Supplement*, 7 July 2006.

3   Smith, A., Wadsworth, E., Moss, S. and Simpson, S. (2004) *The Scale and Impact of Illegal Drug Use by Workers*. London: Health and Safety Executive.

4   *Ibid.*

5   Bird, S.M. (2007) 'Compulsory drug testing in the British Army: Assessing the data.' *Journal of the Royal United Services Institute 152*, 6, 54–9.

6   Gillan, A. (2007) *Army 'losing a battalion a year to drug abuse', The Guardian*, 14 December.

7   Webb, A. (2006) *Soldiers of substance, Soldier Magazine*, April.

8   US Department of Defense press release, November 2001. Washington, D.C.: Department of Defense (available at www.defenselink.mil/news/newsarticle.aspx?id=44417, accessed 21 August 2008).

9   US Department of Defense urinalysis statistics, 2001. Washington, D.C.: Department of Defense.

10   US Department of Defense press release, November 2001. Washington, D.C.: Department of Defense (available at www.defenselink.mil/news/newsarticle.aspx?id=44417, accessed 21 August 2008).

11   About.com: US military (2008) 'The orderly room' (available at http://usmilitary.about.com/od/theorderlyroom/l/bldrugtests2.htm, accessed 19 March 2008).

Chapter Seven

The Global Cannabis Industry

It is not our purpose in writing this book to bombard the reader with endless statistics or to litter each page with figures to support one fact or another. However, in our view, if the reader is to have a good chance of gaining a clear and comprehensive picture of the cannabis scene within their own locality, and an understanding of how that scene fits into the context of the worldwide scene, it is necessary to paint that picture using a number of carefully selected and, most importantly, reliable statistics. The text will direct the interested reader, who may wish to access more detail, to the sources of those statistics that we do use within this chapter, so that they may carry out their own further research.

Cultivation worldwide

Cannabis is today by far the most commonly used illegal drug[1] worldwide. This is particularly true in what is often called the 'developed world'. The United Nations *2007 World Drug Report*[2] estimates the worldwide consumer market for cannabis at 160 million people. This compares with an estimated 1250 million people who smoke tobacco.[3] Cannabis is cultivated on both a small domestic and large commercial scale in almost every user country; indeed, the UN report states that in 2007 at least 172 countries worldwide were involved in cannabis cultivation. Evidence gathered in recent years through the UN Office on Drugs and Crime and the European Monitoring Centre for Drugs and Drug Addiction (EMCDDA) suggests that a number of countries who were in recent times almost exclusively cannabis importers, with only insignificant home-grown cultivation, have begun to evolve into important producers of the drug. This new production is based upon sophisticated indoor hydroponic growing methods producing commercially important quantities of a high-quality and highly potent product that is able to satisfy a growing proportion of that country's domestic market. The topic of hydroponics and its impact on today's cannabis scene will be returned to in more length later in this chapter.

Herbal cannabis production

Gathering figures for the worldwide production of any drug is difficult; after all, cultivating cannabis is an illegal activity attracting serious penalties and producers naturally do not report the outcome of their efforts to the authorities. Best estimates[4] suggest that worldwide herbal cannabis production, following several years of steady increase, peaked in 2004 at 45,000 metric tonnes and then declined in 2005, the last year for which figures are currently available, to 42,000 metric tonnes. Of that total, 26 per cent was produced in Africa, 23 per cent in Central/South America and the Caribbean, 23 per cent in North America, 22 per cent in Asia, 5 per cent (a rise from 3% in 2003) in Europe and 1 per cent in Oceania. To put the quantity of herbal cannabis produced worldwide into perspective, it can be compared with a world production in 2005 of 472 metric tonnes of heroin, 980 metric tonnes of cocaine and over 7 million metric tonnes of tobacco. The total land area used to cultivate herbal cannabis worldwide in 2005 is estimated at 530,000 hectares, compared with approximately 150,000 hectares each for both opium poppies and coca, and 4 million hectares for tobacco.[5] Yields of herbal cannabis per hectare vary according to the weather, the degree of skill of the grower, the quality of the soil, the availability of irrigation, the degree of tending given to the plant, and many other factors. Figures range between 1 and 5 metric tonnes per hectare for outdoor grown plants, and between 15 and 30 metric tonnes per hectare for plants grown hydroponically indoors.

Herbal cannabis potency tends to vary widely as a result of differences in the cultivation methods used, weather conditions and so on. Herbal samples seized in Europe and analyzed in 2004[6] indicated a range of potency of between <1 and 34 per cent, with all of the European countries contributing to the EMCDDA survey reporting an increase in average herbal potency over the previous ten years. Some reports suggest that a similar increase in herbal potency has been occurring in the US;[7] however, historically, potency rates for herbal cannabis in the US have been significantly lower than those found in European countries. As a result, and despite the reported rise, US potency rates in 2004[8] were reported as an average at street level of 5 per cent. The National Drug and Alcohol Research Centre (NDARC) in Sydney, Australia, reported that herbal potency rates for 2007 range between >1 and 20 per cent. No up-to-date potency figures are available for New Zealand, but it seems reasonable to suggest that they will not differ greatly from those found for Australia. Similarly, up-to-date potency figures for South Africa have proved impossible to locate. South Africa is the home for a number of herbal cannabis types, such as *dagga* and *Swazi gold*, which are noted for their high potency and therefore much sought after on the international market.

Cannabis resin production

UN estimates indicate that resin production has fallen worldwide from a 2004 figure of 7500 metric tonnes to a 2005 figure of 6600 metric tonnes. The production of cannabis resin on a commercial scale is far less global than that of herbal cannabis, and the outdoor cultivation of cannabis plants specifically for conversion to resin occurs in only a small number of countries, chiefly Morocco, Afghanistan, Pakistan, India, Lebanon, Albania and Jamaica.

Morocco remains the most important country in the production of cannabis resin, with between a quarter and a third of user countries reporting that Morocco was its primary source of illegally imported resin. Indeed, estimates vary, but something in the region of 70 per cent of the resin smuggled into Western Europe originates in Morocco. However, in the past few years the Moroccan government has been involved in strenuous efforts to reduce the country's involvement in the cannabis trade. They report that the area under cannabis production within their borders has fallen from a 2003 figure of 134,000 hectares to a 2005 figure of 72,500 hectares, with a resulting fall in resin production from 3060 metric tonnes to 1066 metric tonnes. It is highly likely that this fall in cannabis cultivation in Morocco has contributed significantly to the fall seen worldwide in resin production. It is worth noting that the decline in cannabis resin production worldwide would perhaps have been even greater, but for an increase in the land area devoted to its cultivation in Afghanistan from 30,000 hectares in 2004 to 50,000 hectares in 2005.

Potency rates for cannabis resin vary as widely as they do for the herbal variety, again as a result of the cultivation methods used for the source plants, and the techniques used in producing the resin. In 2004[9] reported resin potency in Europe varied between <1 and 49 per cent, with the majority of European countries contributing to the EMCDDA survey reporting a steady increase in resin potency over the previous ten years. Potency figures for resin in the US[10] in 2004 indicate an average THC content of around 11 per cent, the highest figure since records began, rising to 28 per cent by 2007. The NDARC reports 2007 potency figures for resin in Australia of between 10 and 20 per cent.

No up-to-date potency figures are available for New Zealand but it seems reasonable to suggest that they will not differ greatly from those found for Australia. Similarly, no potency figures for resin in South Africa are currently available.

Cannabis oil production

Details of the global picture of cannabis oil production are very difficult to come by. Reports from drug agencies, such as the US Drug Enforcement Administration (DEA), Interpol and the UN Office on Drugs and Crime, indicate that the conversion of herbal or resin cannabis into the highly potent oil form occurs almost exclusively on a small-scale basis. The global amount produced is minute in comparison with herbal or resin cannabis production, and tends to take place in the user countries themselves (see seizure figures later in this chapter as an illustration of the size of this market). Cannabis oil has the potential to contain the highest levels of THC found in any variety of the drug.

Oil potency figures for the UK[11] for 2004 indicate a THC content of between 25 and 45 per cent, whilst figures for the US, for 2004,[12] indicate a potency level of between 43 and 75 per cent. The figure for Australia[13] in 2007 lay between 15 and 30 per cent.

Global cannabis seizures

Enforcement efforts by the legal authorities in the UK, the US and a number of other countries will be dealt with individually later in this chapter, but we think it useful to the reader to first present the global picture, so that they are able to place the actions taken and the results obtained within their own localities in a wider context.

Cannabis remains the most commonly smuggled drug worldwide[14] and accounts for over half of all drug seizures made by customs and law enforcement officers. The UN Office on Drugs and Crime reports that a total of 4600 metric tonnes of herbal cannabis was intercepted and seized in 2005, representing a little under 11 per cent of the estimated total global production. Resin seizures amounted to 1300 metric tonnes in 2005, a little under 20 per cent of estimated production. As stated earlier, it is impossible to obtain any reliable estimate of global production of cannabis oil. However, based on the estimated percentage seizure rates for both herbal and resin cannabis, the total amount of oil seized in 2005 of some 700 litres would indicate a global production figure of around 5000 litres.

All three 2005 seizure figures indicate a decline in tonnage (herbal -35%, rcsin -11%, oil -5%) over the same figures for 2004. Cannabis seizure figures can be interpreted as merely a reflection of the effort put into anti-trafficking measures from one year to the next, together with the skill and cunning of traffickers, and/or the luck experienced by the smugglers and the authorities. However, it is also perhaps reasonable to interpret the decline in the global weight of cannabis seized as being a reflection of a small decline in the global market.

It is worth spending just a little longer looking at global seizure figures as they can tell us a lot about which type of cannabis is most popular in different world regions. Around 64 per cent of all the herbal cannabis seized globally was in North America, 18 per cent in Africa, 2 per cent in Europe and <1 per cent in Oceania. Seizures of resin are dominated by Europe, with 71 per cent of the global total; in Africa it is 8 per cent, <1 per cent for North America and an insignificant level in Oceania (around 2 kg only seized in 2005). Quite clearly it is reasonable to deduce from the seizure figures that in Europe resin occupies the top spot in the cannabis scene, whilst in the US and in Oceania the market is plainly dominated by herbal cannabis.

National cannabis scenes

The United Kingdom

As with all of the countries profiled in this chapter, cannabis is the most common illegal drug used in the UK with some 3 million users.[15] Statistics published by the EMCDDA indicate that 117,783 people in the UK sought treatment for drug-related problems in 2005, and that 52.8 per cent gave cannabis as their primary drug of use.

Cannabis sativa can be, and is, grown in the open in the UK, but it does not flourish in the temperate and somewhat unpredictable climate. We have personally seen cannabis plants cultivated in 'grow-bags' set against south-facing garden walls, in vegetable plots, in garden greenhouses and, on one occasion, at the top of an embankment alongside a busy main road. This last example had been planted by a local user who thought it safer to grow his plants away from home. He had reasoned that by doing so he would only be at risk of discovery whilst planting them, and again when the time came for him to harvest them. He had not counted on the unpredictability of the British weather. A prolonged period of drought and hot weather necessitated his visiting the plants on a daily basis to water them. His daily walks along the main road, carrying a heavy container of water, were noted by a suspicious police traffic officer who followed him to his 'plantation'. A prosecution then ensued.

In almost all cases of cannabis grown outside in the UK, the THC levels will generally be very low. To obtain commercially acceptable levels of THC, it is necessary to provide the high light levels and warm temperatures that mimic the plant's natural home artificially.

The UK indoor growing scene

The indoor growing of cannabis in the UK has, in recent years, taken off in popularity. Cannabis has been grown indoors in the UK for many decades, but most of this was on a very small scale, sometimes only a plant or two grown on a bedroom windowsill. Occasionally someone would attempt to increase the scale of their enterprise, and turn a whole room into a growing area, with special daylight-imitating lights, heaters and either grow-bags or pots of soil.

Even more rarely, one could come across examples where hydroponic growing techniques were utilized. Hydroponics takes advantage of the way all plants grow. They feed by absorbing nutrients in the form of particles suspended in water, with the soil acting as a reservoir of such particles and the necessary water, but playing no direct part in nourishing the plant. Clearly how fertile a particular soil is depends on the level of nutrient particles and water it contains. The main role of soil in the growing process is to provide support for the plant, with the plant spreading out its root system, not only to take in nutrients, but also to support its growth above ground. In hydroponic growing methods, the soil is replaced by inert substances such as gravel, mineral wool (such as that used in house insulation) and perlite. These media provide the reservoir for the water-borne nutrients, and some measure of plant support. In more sophisticated hydroponic techniques, the inert medium is done away with completely, and the plant roots encouraged to spread themselves directly within a container of nutrient liquid. In both techniques plant support is provided artificially.

A quick search of the Internet reveals literally thousands of websites eager to sell hydroponic growing equipment with no questions asked. Most are able to supply daylight spectrum lights, heaters, fans, growing medium, nutrients, computer-controlled timers, supports and even chambers to optimize humidity. Many thousands of other websites are devoted to providing information, tips and guidance to potential hydroponic cannabis growers.

The near-perfect growing conditions achievable through hydroponic techniques allow the grower to achieve both high yields and high potency, making it a very attractive proposition to specialize in such cannabis types as skunk and super-skunk. These forms of cannabis have been produced by interbreeding

Cannabis sativa and *Cannabis indica*, with the most potent skunk plants achieved through a 75 per cent *sativa* to 25 per cent *indica* hybrid. Once a good high-yield and high-potency hybrid plant is produced, it is then cloned by growers to produce seed that will germinate true, and produce endless quantities of high-yield and high-potency skunk plants.

Another quick search of the Internet will reveal thousands of websites that specialize in the sale of skunk plant seeds. The easy availability of equipment, seeds and knowledge regarding the technique has led to an explosion in such enterprises. In the two-year period up to March 2007, the Metropolitan Police in London closed down some 1500 hydroponic cannabis 'farmhouses', each containing on average some 400 plants. This was three times the number closed down in the previous two-year period.

Organized crime and hydroponics

As described earlier in this chapter, statistics gathered in the UK indicate that, in 2004 and 2005, around 3 million[16] 16–59-year-olds used cannabis in one form or another, representing an enormous user market with the potential for the yielding of vast profits. Resin remains the most popular form of cannabis in the UK, with herbal coming a close second and cannabis oil occupying a very small third place. Until recent times, the vast majority of cannabis of all kinds used in the UK was imported, with perhaps <10 per cent of the market being satisfied by domestic cultivation. This 'home-grown' would have generally been low in potency, and would not have been ideal for the production of resin or conversion into oil. It would have provided only a rather weak form of herbal cannabis.

Now, however, the situation is very different, with the drug information organization DrugScope reporting that in 2007 the proportion of the UK market in cannabis that was produced within the UK had risen to <60 per cent, with this being used to supply the herbal market (mostly in the form of skunk), the resin market, and the still small oil market.

A typical hydroponic cannabis 'farm' in the UK will involve the conversion of an entire house. Rooms will have their windows blacked out, and their walls and ceiling insulated. High-power daylight-spectrum lights, fans and heaters will then be installed, along with the required hydroponic growing equipment. The cost of converting a typical domestic house to an efficient cannabis 'farm' is estimated in 2008 to be somewhere between £20,000 and £25,000. However, the potential profits from a 'farm', housing 200 cannabis plants, can be as high as £30,000[17] in the first three months.

One of the ways in which enforcement agencies detect the presence of such an establishment is through the high electricity consumption of the lights, fans and heaters, etc. Electricity supply agencies in the UK co-operate with the police in reporting such excessively high consumption. To avoid being detected in this way, many 'indoor farmers' will bypass the house electricity meters and connect illegally directly to the mains supply. Examples have been seen where connections have even been made to local street lighting! Clearly such activities carry with them high fire and electrocution risks. Indeed, in 2006, some 50 cannabis 'farms' were detected in London[18] directly as a result of them catching fire.

The prospect of vast profits to be made has attracted the attention of many groups of organized criminals. On 25 September 2006, the UK police launched Operation Keymer specifically to target such enterprises. This operation ran for only 11 days, and led to hundreds of suspected houses being raided. The police[19] report that from these houses a total of 133 people were arrested and over 28,000 cannabis plants and 54 kg of prepared resin seized and destroyed. Under UK legislation allowing the confiscation of drug financed assets, the police also seized £160,000 in cash, four houses and a number of expensive motor cars.

Reports in many newspapers have drawn attention to the increasing involvement of organized criminal groups from Vietnam in this trade. Indeed, analysis of the results of raids on cannabis farms across the country[20] by different police forces indicates that between 60 and 75 per cent of UK farms are operated by criminals of Vietnamese nationality. In September 2007, the drug charity DrugScope released a press briefing drawing attention to 'The plight of Vietnamese children caught up in illegal cannabis cultivation in this country'.[21] An investigation mounted by the charity revealed that large numbers of Vietnamese children, some aged as young as 14, have been smuggled into the UK as illegal immigrants to act as minders for indoor cannabis farms. The children act as what DrugScope call 'human sprinkler systems', tending to the needs of the plants whilst living within the house in what can only be called appalling conditions. Examples have been seen of such children living in cupboards under the stairs, on mattresses in hallways, or in tiny spaces in the attic, in order to maximize the space available for growing plants. These children are often left in sole charge of the 'farmhouse', and are responsible for operating the lighting and heating system with its potentially dangerous electricity supply, whilst running high risks of fire and electrocution. Because of their status as illegal immigrants, such children have no protection in law and DrugScope describes their position as being akin to 'modern slavery'.

The legal consequences of being found in charge of such a 'farmhouse' when it is raided by the police can be illustrated by drawing upon a case study quoted in a Home Office report of June 2007.[22] The case study refers to a female orphaned child from south-east Asia, her age is not given. She was sold by her guardian to an agent who told her he would send her to the UK so that she would be able to lead a better life. She was then smuggled overland to the French coast and then to the UK, with this arduous journey taking around a year to complete. The first time she came to the notice of the authorities was when she was arrested in a raid on a cannabis 'farmhouse'. Still believing that the agent and others involved in bringing her to the UK were her friends, she did not give any incriminating evidence about them to the police. She was sentenced by the courts to a term of imprisonment. The report goes on to state that, although this case study refers to a female child, evidence suggests that the majority of children trafficked into the UK to tend cannabis farms are males.

The Home Office reports that Vietnamese adults as well as children are being smuggled into the country. These adults are often in 'debt bondage' to the traffickers, and therefore under strict obligation to carry out their instructions. The traffickers in effect sell these 'slaves' to the criminal gangs operating the cannabis 'farmhouses'. The Home Office report recognizes the vulnerable position of the adults and children, and also their lack of choice over their involvement in the cultivation of cannabis. It has advised the police and Crown Prosecution Service that adults and children found in such circumstances should no longer be arrested and prosecuted as offenders, but rather seen as victims in need of help.

It is worth concluding this section on the involvement of organized criminal gangs in cannabis cultivation by quoting Martin Barnes, the chief executive of DrugScope, who, on the issuing of the press briefing referred to earlier, stated:

> Some have considered large scale cannabis cultivation as an almost 'victimless crime' but the reality is that vulnerable young people are being exploited. Unfortunately they find themselves victims twice over, both at the hands of the criminal gangs who brought them to this country, forcing them to work in cramped dangerous conditions to fuel the illegal drug trade, and again when they find themselves treated as criminals by the UK authorities.

The United States

In the US, common with almost all other countries, cannabis is the most commonly used illegal drug. The UN Office on Drugs and Crime[23] report that in 2005 some 12.6 per cent of Americans between the ages of 15 and 64 had used cannabis within the previous year. Of the more than 2,000,000 people in the US treated for drug problems in 2005, almost half of them reported that their primary drug of use was cannabis. Herbal cannabis, much more usually referred to as marijuana, is by far the most common form of cannabis used in the US.

Resin cannabis is referred to as hash or hashish, and represents a small part of the overall market. Some cannabis oil is seen, but it remains very much a minority product amongst cannabis users.

The DEA[24] reported in 2008 that the demand by cannabis users for much higher potency levels was continuing. The use by the authorities of aircraft, and even ground mapping satellites, to search for commercial production of cannabis in the open air, has led to a rapid increase in production indoors. Large-scale cultivation outdoors is now seen as unsafe, with US law enforcement agencies seizing and destroying almost 6 million outdoor grown plants in 2006.[25] As a bonus, indoor cultivation using similar high-tech methods as those found in the UK has led to substantial increases in the potency of the cannabis produced.

The combination of these two factors has led to the development of a increasing market for the high-potency product. The profit potential represented by such a market has attracted the attentions of what the DEA calls DTOs (drug-trafficking organizations): in other words, organized criminal gangs. In a picture very similar to that seen in the UK, many of these indoor cannabis production facilities are operated by organized Vietnamese gangs. Competition for this market is fierce and large numbers of organized Mexican and Cuban criminals are also involved.

Canada

Canada represents a substantial market for cannabis. The Royal Canadian Mounted Police, in a review of crime in 2007,[26] estimated that some 14 per cent of the total Canadian population had used the drug in 2004. This is a very crude measure of the nature of the cannabis scene, but the report also states that 30 per cent of Canadians aged between 15 and 17 years, and 47 per cent of those aged 18 and 19 years, claimed to use the drug on a daily basis. These figures suggest a large and also highly active market. The UN report that a little over 29,000 Canadians received treatment for problem drug use in 2001. Of these, around 25 per cent gave their primary drug as cannabis. The same demand for high potency, seen elsewhere, exists, and thus a thriving indoor cannabis market has developed, with Quebec and Ontario producing over 50 per cent of the nation's crop. Again it is organized criminal groups who control most of this trade, and again Vietnamese gangs feature greatly in this. Much of the cannabis produced indoors in Canada is exported to the US, with the Royal Canadian Mounted Police estimating, in 2007, that this export trade was worth around C$5 billion to the criminal gangs involved.

Australia

As with all of the countries so far profiled, cannabis is the most common illegal drug in use in Australia.[27] According to a national survey published in 2005 by the Australian Institute of Health and Welfare, cannabis use in Australia continues to fall and has declined to an 11-year low. The survey estimates that some 295,000 Australians use cannabis on a daily basis, and another 410,000 at least once a week. In the 12 months up to June 2004, some 71,800 Australians received treatment for drug-related problems, with 39.6 per cent stating that cannabis was their primary drug.[28] Herbal is by far the most popular form of the drug, with around 85 per cent of Australian users stating a preference for it over resin.[29]

The home cannabis industry is strong enough to supply this domestic demand, and to undercut imports on price. Cannabis is cultivated in every state and territory in Australia, and whilst large outdoor areas of growing cannabis (bush plots) are still discovered on as regular basis, the move in recent times has been towards indoor growing, with an increasing use being made of hydroponics. The Australian Crime Commission reports that, whilst there is clear evidence of a growing involvement in cannabis cultivation by organized criminal gangs, no single group has been able to achieve any position of dominance. In a reflection of the trends found in the other countries, there is evidence of Vietnamese/Australian criminals travelling to Canada to further their knowledge of hydroponic techniques, and then returning with that knowledge to strengthen the Australian cannabis industry.

New Zealand

As in the other profiled countries, cannabis occupies the top spot in terms of illegal drug popularity in New Zealand.[30] Survey findings for 2003 estimate that around 4 per cent of 15–45-year-olds use cannabis at least ten times each month, and another 4 per cent use on a daily basis. If that figure has remained stable then, based on 2006 population figures, some 144,000 New Zealanders are regular users of cannabis. In 2005 around 3900 New Zealanders received treatment for drug problems, with 53 per cent of them giving cannabis as their primary drug.[31] By far the commonest form of cannabis used in New Zealand is herbal, but the trends would suggest that the use of resin is beginning to increase. As with Australia, the cannabis market in New Zealand is serviced almost totally by domestically grown cannabis, and the same picture of a move from outdoor to indoor cultivation is apparent. Also apparent is the growing involvement of organized criminal groups in exactly the same way as seen in the other profiled countries.

South Africa

Again cannabis is the most popular illegal drug in South Africa, with an estimated 8.9 per cent of 15–64-year-old South Africans using it during 2005.[32] Of the 14,700 people receiving treatment for drug problems in 2005, some 34 per cent gave cannabis as their primary drug. Figures released in November 2007[33] estimated that, for people under 20 years of age seeking drug treatment, that figure rose to over 50 per cent. Herbal cannabis is by far the most popular form of the drug in use. Herbal cannabis is often referred to as 'dagga' in South Africa, but this can be confusing as another plant, *Leonotis leonurus*, known as 'wild dagga', also smoked or brewed into tea for its narcotic effect.

Also popular in South Africa is a mix of cannabis and the prescription drug Mandrax, known as *white pipe*, which is usually smoked. Mandrax was developed as a sedative and aid to sleep, and contains Methaqualone as its primary ingredient. Its use with cannabis represents a number of potentially serious additional problems for the user, as compared with cannabis alone. The South African Ministry of Health issues a fact leaflet on using cannabis in combination with Mandrax, which the interested reader can access on: www.sahealthinfo.org/admodule/cannabis.htm.

South Africa is a major producer of cannabis, with a 2005 crop estimated at 2200 metric tonnes.[34] This is sufficient to service all its domestic needs and allows for a considerable export trade, much of which is destined for Europe.

The South African drug enforcement agencies are very active, placing the country in third place in the global cannabis seizures league for both 2004, with 818 metric tonnes, and 2005, with 292 metric tonnes.

There are as yet no reports of any major move from outdoor to indoor cultivation, and no reports of any significant involvement of organized criminal groups in the way we have seen in the other countries profiled.

Notes

1   Earleywine, M. (2005) *Understanding Marijuana.* Oxford: Oxford University Press; Julien, R.M. (2005) *A Primer of Drug Action: Tenth Edition.* New York: Worth Publishers.

2   UN Office on Drugs and Crime (2007) *2007 World Drug Report.*

3   *The Tobacco Atlas,* World Health Organization (available at www.who.int/tobacco/resources/publications/tobacco_atlas/en/index.html, accessed 22 August 2008).

4   UN Office on Drugs and Crime (2007) *2007 World Drug Report.*

5   *The Tobacco Atlas*, World Health Organization (available at www.who.int/tobacco/resources/publications/tobacco_atlas/en/index.html, accessed 22 August 2008).

6   Potency of cannabis products at retail level, The European Monitoring Centre for Drugs and Drug Addiction, 2004, (available at http://stats06.emcdda.europa.eu/en/elements/pptabs05a-en.html, accessed 22 August 2008).

7   ElSohly, M.A., Ross, S.A., Mehmedic, Z., Arafat, R., Yi, B. and Banahan, B. (2000) 'Potency trends of delta-9-THC and other cannabinoids in confiscated marijuana from 1980–1997.' *Journal of Forensic Science 45*, 1, 24–30.

8   UN Office on Drugs and Crime (2006) *2006 World Drug Report*.

9   The European Monitoring Centre for Drugs and Drug Addiction (2006) 'Drug availability and drug markets: prices and purity information.' (available at http://stats06.emcdda.europa.eu/en/elements/pptabs05a-en.html, accessed 22 August 2008).

10   ElSohly, M.A. (2004) 'NIDA Marijuana Potency Monitoring Project Quarterly Report number 87.' Lafayette, MS: University of Mississippi; ElSohly, M.A. (2008) 'NIDA Marijuana Potency Monitoring Project Quarterly Report number 100.' Lafayette, MS: University of Mississippi.

11   The European Monitoring Centre for Drugs and Drug Addiction (2004) *EMCDDA Insights: An Overview of Cannabis Potency in Europe* Lisbon: The European Monitoring Centre for Drugs and Drug Addiction.

12   UN Office on Drugs and Crime (2006) *2006 World Drug Report*.

13   National Drug and Alcohol Research Centre, Sydney, Australia. *Factsheet* (available at http://ndarc.med.unswedu.au/NDARCWeb.nsf/resources/NDARCFact_Drugs4/$file/CANNABIS+POTENCY+FACT+SHEET.pdf, accessed 12 June 2008).

14   Interpol: Cannabis (available at www.interpol.int/public/Drugs/cannabis/default.asp, accessed 22 August 2008).

15   DrugScope UK 'Cannabis' (available at www.drugscope.org.uk/resources/drugsearch/drugsearchpages/cannabs.htm, accessed 12 June 2008).

16   DrugScope, UK. (available at www.drugscope.org.uk/resources/drugsearch/ drugsearchpages/cannabs.htm, accessed 12 June 2008).

17   Association of Chief Police Officers (ACPO) 'Operation Keymer – nipping cannabis cultivation in the bud.' 25 September 2006, UK (available at http://www.acpo.police.uk/pressrelease.asp?PR_GUID=%7B8ADB07A1-0FB9-41EA-8C52-75DBC865708A%7D, accessed 22 August 2008).

18   London Fire Brigade. 'DrugScope reveals child victims of UK cannabis farm boom.' 6 September 2007 (available at http://www.drugscope.org.uk/ourwork/pressoffice/pressreleases/Cannabis-farms-trafficked-children.htm, accessed 22 August 2008).

19   UK ACPO. 'ACPO response to DrugScope report concerning cannabis cultivation.' 13 March 2007, ACPO press release (available at http://www.acpo.police.uk/asp/news/PRDisplay.asp?PR_GUID={36FDC041-0677-4C91-AC4D-BF7BB8AD1632}, accessed 22 August 2008).

20   London Fire Brigade. 'DrugScope reveals child victims of UK cannabis farm boom.' 6 September 2007 (available at http://www.drugscope.org.uk/ourwork/pressoffice/pressreleases/Cannabis-farms-trafficked-children.htm, accessed 22 August 2008).

21   DrugScope (2007) 'DrugScope reveals child victims of UK cannabis farm boom'. Press release, 6 September.

22   UK Home Office (2007) *A Scoping Project on Child Trafficking in the UK*. London: Home Office.

23   UN Office on Drugs and Crime (2007) *2007 World Drug Report*.

24   National Drugs Intelligence Centre (2007) *National Drug Threat Assessment 2008*, US Department of Justice (available at www.usdoj.gov/ndic/pubs25/25921/25921p.pdf, accessed 22 August 2008).

25   UN Office on Drugs and Crime (2007) *2007 World Drug Report*.

26   Royal Canadian Mounted Police (2007) *2007 Environmental Scan* (available at www.rcmpgrc.gc.ca/enviro/2007index_e.htm, accessed 12 June 2008.

27   Australian Crime Commission (2007) *Illicit Drug Data Report 2005–2006* (available at www.crimecommission.gov.au/html/pg_iddr2005-06.html, accessed 12 June 2008).

28   UN Office of Drugs and Crime (2006) *2006 World Drug Report.*

29   Australian Institute of Health and Welfare (2005) *National Drug Strategy Household Survey – deleted findings* (available at www.aihw.gov.au/publications/index.cfm/title/10190, accessed 12 June 2008).

30   New Zealand Ministry of Health (2007) *National Drug Policy New Zealand* (available at www.ndp.govt.nz/moh.nsf/indexcm/npd-publications-nationaldrugpolicy 20072012?Open, accessed 12 June 2008).

31   UN Office on Drugs and Crime (2006) *2006 World Drug Report.*

32   UN Office on Drugs and Crime (2007) *2007 World Drug Report.*

33   South African Community Epidemiology Network on Drug Use (2007) *Alcohol and Drug Trends January–June 2007* (available at www.sahealthinfo.org/admodule/sacendunov2007.pdf, accessed 12 June 2008).

34   UN Office on Drugs and Crime (2006) *2006 World Drug Report.*

Chapter Eight

Cannabis and the Law

There are no countries around the world that we are aware of where the criminal law ignores cannabis. Even in those countries which take a 'liberal' view of the use of cannabis, the law still lays out exactly where the limits of its liberal approach are, and exactly what is permitted and what is not. It is perhaps worth pausing for a moment to consider why this should be so. Why should a naturally occurring plant attract so much legal attention? This a question that we will return to later in this chapter.

It is not possible, or indeed particularly useful, in a book such as this, to detail the whole mass of international law on this subject. Rather, this chapter will attempt to set out the major landmarks in the history of the involvement of the criminal law with cannabis, and to provide you with some guidance as to where to check out the current legal situation regarding the drug in a number of different countries.

Laws on drugs in general, and cannabis in particular, can be very complex and subject to fairly frequent change, particularly in the manner and intensity of their enforcement. Breaches of drug laws can bring serious and long-lasting consequences for the perpetrator. You are strongly advised to confirm the up-to-date position with the legal authorities in your locality, especially before undertaking any potentially risky behaviour.

Early legal steps in cannabis legislation

This volume focuses solely on cannabis, but it is necessary to make a short diversion into the legal history of opium in order to uncover the start of the modern pattern of legal controls over cannabis. At The Hague in Holland in January

1912, the International Opium Commission, set up by the US in 1909, met to agree an international convention seeking to control the increasing misuse of opium. The International Opium Convention was signed and ratified by a number of Western countries, including the UK, the US, Germany, France and Holland, and by a number of Eastern countries, including China, Japan, Russia and Thailand. Signatory countries were then under obligation to introduce laws in their own territories to control opium misuse.

The League of Nations

The International Opium Convention of 1912 came under the authority of the newly formed League of Nations, set up under the Treaty of Versailles in 1919 which marked the formal end of the First World War. This meant that countries who became members of the League were obliged also to introduce opium control legislation. The 1912 Convention was subject to extensive revision in 1925, and cannabis was for the first time also included. In its original draft the new International Convention on Narcotics Control required signatory countries to outlaw completely all non-medical use of cannabis but, following a number of objections from countries where ritual use of the drug was common, the mandatory nature of the Convention was softened. In its revised form the Convention allowed countries to exempt themselves from the requirement to outlaw all non-medical use, whilst still requiring them to take all possible steps to control the traffic in cannabis between member countries.

The United Kingdom

As a result of the revised Convention, the UK government in 1925 passed into law the Dangerous Drugs Act which amended a previous drug law of 1920 to include 'Indian hemp, and resins obtained from Indian hemp and all preparations of which such resins form the base'. Indian hemp was further defined as 'the dried flowering or fruiting tops of the pistillate plant known as Cannabis Sativa, from which the resin has not been extracted, by whatever name such tops are called'. The section of this Act dealing with cannabis came into force in 1928 and, for the first time in the UK, the cultivation, possession and supply of the drug became a criminal offence.

The British Empire and Commonwealth countries

By the end of the 1920s, the majority of countries within the British Empire and Commonwealth of Nations, including Australia, Canada, New Zealand and South Africa, together with a number of countries across Western Europe, had enacted almost identical laws controlling the misuse of cannabis.

The United States

The legal situation in the US was fundamentally different to that in the UK. The US, for political reasons, was never a member of the League of Nations, and was thus not subject to the requirements of the 1925 International Convention on Narcotics Control. Legal control of cannabis in the US, therefore, followed a different route.

In the early years of the twentieth century, a growing number of states, starting with California in 1915, introduced laws controlling the non-medical use of cannabis and other drugs. In 1930 the US federal government formed the Federal Bureau of Narcotics and one its first jobs was to attempt to rationalize the existing patchwork of drug legislation across the US, with the passing of the Uniform Narcotic Drug Act. This was intended to provide a set of model laws for states to adopt, and designed to enforce the complete prohibition of *Cannabis sativa* and *indica* and any derivatives of them, along with a number of other drugs. This Act still left the individual states with the responsibility for framing their own prohibition legislation, but a small number of them still took no action. As a result, in 1937, the US federal government enacted the Marijuana Tax Act which made it a federal offence to cultivate or to supply cannabis without a government-issued tax stamp. The federal government had no intention of making such stamps available and had in effect made the trade in cannabis unlawful across the whole of the US. Within the nationwide umbrella provided by the Marijuana Tax Act, individual states were still left to enforce their own cannabis legislation covering offences such as possession and use.

Thus, by the end of the 1930s, the majority of countries worldwide came to consider the non-medical use of cannabis as a criminal matter, with a wide range of serious penalties available for any offenders.

The United Nations

The international legal situation remained largely stable until the beginning of the 1960s. The League of Nations had by now been replaced by the UN who, as part of its international health remit, had formed the International Narcotics

Control Board. In 1961 a total of 73 countries met at UN headquarters in New York to consider an update to the 1925 International Convention on Narcotics Control. Their deliberations resulted in the Single Convention on Narcotic Drugs.[1] Before setting out the results of this piece of international legislation, it is worth looking for a moment at the intentions of this Convention. Below are the actual words of the preamble to the final document, and they provide a clear picture of the rationale for the legislation agreed upon by the attending countries (the italics are those of the UN):

> *The Parties,*
>
> *Concerned* with the health and welfare of mankind,
>
> *Recognizing* that the medical use of narcotic drugs continues to be indispensable for the relief of pain and suffering and that adequate provision must be made to ensure the availability of narcotic drugs for such purposes,
>
> *Recognizing* that addiction to narcotic drugs constitutes a serious evil for the individual and is fraught with social and economic danger to mankind,
>
> *Conscious* of their duty to prevent and combat this evil,
>
> *Considering* that effective measures against abuse of narcotic drugs require co-ordinated and universal action,
>
> *Understanding* that such universal action calls for international co-operation guided by the same principles and aimed at common objectives,
>
> *Acknowledging* the competence of the United Nations in the field of narcotics control and desirous that the international organs concerned should be within the framework of that Organization,
>
> *Desiring* to conclude a generally acceptable international convention replacing existing treaties on narcotic drugs, limiting such drugs to medical and scientific use, and providing for continuous international co-operation and control for the achievement of such aims and objectives, hereby agree:

The thinking and intentions that are evident in this preamble may go some way towards answering the question posed at the start of this chapter as to the reasons, mistaken or not, for laws controlling the non-medical use of drugs such as cannabis.

The enactment of the 1961 Single Convention on Narcotic Drugs placed upon member states of the UN the obligation to enact legislation within their own borders to prohibit the cultivation, manufacture, trafficking and use, other than for scientific or medical purposes, of a number of drugs, including cannabis in all its forms. Member states were also obliged to provide a high level of co-operation with each other to make such a prohibition as effective as possible. The 1961 Convention was amended in 1972 to add to and reinforce the parts of the original Convention that obliged member states to recognize the links between social deprivation and problem drug use, and to take steps to deal with such deprivation, and to provide treatment services for drug users.

Current national cannabis laws

The websites below may prove useful for anyone seeking detailed information regarding cannabis laws in different countries.

The United States of America

The US has both federal and state law-making bodies, and cannabis control laws vary widely. Basically it is true to say that all cultivation, trafficking, possession and use of cannabis in the US is controlled by law. Cannabis for non-medical use is not available without legal restriction anywhere in the US. The following website maintained by the National Organization for the Reform of Marijuana Laws (NORML) provides state-by-state information on cannabis laws: www.norml.org/index.cfm?Group_ID=4516 (accessed 22 August 2008)

The United Kingdom

The law is applied on a nationwide basis. The legal classification of cannabis has been subject to a number of changes in recent years. The following website provides details of the current position:
    www.drugscope.org.uk/resources/drugsearch/drugsearchpages/cannabis.htm (accessed 13 June 2008)

Australia

The law is applied on a state and territory basis. The following website provides details of Australian cannabis laws:
    www.druginfo.adf.org.au/article.asp?ContentID=cannabis_law_australia (accessed 13 June 2008)

New Zealand

The law is applied on a nationwide basis. The following website provides information on the drug and its use in New Zealand, and the laws and penalties that apply to it:

www.nzdf.org.nz/cannabis (accessed 13 June 2008)

Canada

The law is applied on a nationwide basis and includes different penalties for differing amounts of the drug. The following website provides a breakdown of the law and penalties:

www.cfdp.ca/law.htm (accessed 13 June 2008)

Should the legal status of cannabis be changed?

For many years now, a number of organizations and individuals have campaigned in various ways for the laws controlling cannabis use to be relaxed, or indeed revoked completely. Entering the search term 'cannabis legalization' into an Internet search engine will reveal a vast number of websites maintained by organizations across the world who campaign for cannabis law reform. The arguments raised by proponents of this view are many and varied, and approach the issue from a number of standpoints. It is not our intention in this book to suggest to you which arguments you should believe and which you should not. Rather, it our hope that you will weigh up the *evidence* offered by such organizations, together with that discussed in this book and to be found elsewhere, and then carefully make your own mind up.

It is perhaps worth saying at the conclusion of this short chapter on the law and cannabis that the legal position of any particular drug is not the only factor that any prospective user should think about. Whether a drug is legal or not, whether it is the subject of only minor controls or draconian ones, should not be the major reason why anyone should or should not use the drug. Any prospective user should carefully weigh up all of the factors involved, including the legal position, but also the immediate and long-term physical and mental health implications; the habituation potential; the cost, social, education and career implications; and many other factors. Then, and only then, can anyone make a truly informed decision regarding cannabis.

Notes

1   The interested reader can find a link to the full text of the 1961 Convention at www.incb.org/incb/convention_1961.html, accessed 7 August 2008.

Conclusions

Whether you have read this book as a concerned parent, a health professional, a current cannabis user, a prospective user or someone seeking to increase and develop their knowledge on this subject, we hope that we have covered sufficient ground to allow you to be better informed about all aspects of this complex subject. We hope, too, that this book may encourage you to investigate the subject further, and to keep up to date with future developments, as undoubtedly there is still much to be discovered and understood about cannabis and its use.

Throughout the book we have attempted to present information in as balanced a manner as possible without unduly influencing you towards any particular conclusions. However, it is apparent to us that whilst accepting that, many users of cannabis will enjoy doing so without coming to any perceived harm, there are those for whom use of the drug will lead to serious consequences, including mental and physical health difficulties, social, legal, employment, educational and relationship problems. Whilst it is true that discontinuation of use of the drug may result in many of these problems abating, it is also true to say that many will be long-lasting or even permanent. Whilst accepting that it is often difficult for young people to think of themselves as getting older, it is our wish that this book may enable current and prospective users of the drug to seriously consider the potential long-term outcomes of such use.

The use of cannabis is illegal to one extent or another in almost every country in the world. Because of its popularity, an enormous worldwide market for the drug has developed, resulting in the potential for vast profits to be made by those servicing this need. This has led to the global cannabis industry being almost totally dominated by organized criminal gangs, with all of the social evils that such involvement brings with it. This negative aspect of cannabis production and distribution should also be considered by end users of the drug.

On an optimistic note, research continues to examine ways in which cannabis and derivatives from it can be exploited medicinally to bring benefits in the treatment of an increasing range of health problems. We are confident that such beneficial uses will be found, but pharmaceutical applications of the drug will involve using cannabis in very different forms and ways to those in which the drug is commonly used for recreational purposes.

Appendix One

Glossary of Terms

Adulterants:	A wide range of substances added to cannabis either to add weight or to change its appearance.
Cannabinoids:	A range of complex chemicals produced by the cannabis plant, some of which have psychoactive properties.
Cannabis indica:	One of the three main varieties of the drug-producing cannabis plant.
Cannabis oil:	An oil with a high THC content, produced by mixing either cannabis resin or plant material with a solvent such as grain alcohol, denatured alcohol, naptha, acetone, etc.
Cannabis resin:	A solid form of the drug, produced by collecting, drying and pressing the resinous exudate of the cannabis plant, particularly the female plant.
Cannabis ruderalis:	One of the three main varieties of the drug-producing cannabis plant.
Cannabis sativa:	The most important of the three main varieties of the drug-producing cannabis plant.
Chillum pipe:	A pipe designed to reduce the temperature of cannabis smoke.
Cognitive behavioural therapy:	A form of psychotherapy based on modifying cognitions, assumptions, beliefs and behaviours, with the aim of alleviating disturbed emotions.
DEA:	The Drug Enforcement Administration. A department of the US federal government tasked to enforce the controlled substances laws and regulations of the US.
$\Delta 9$ Tetrahydrocannabinol:	The most psychoactive of the cannabinoids, known as THC.
Depersonalization:	A change in an individual's self-awareness such that they feel detached from their own experience, with the self, their body, and mind seeming alien.
Depression:	Emotional state characterized by sadness, unhappy thoughts, apathy and dejection.
Derealization:	A change in an individual's experience of the environment, where the world around them feels unreal and unfamiliar.
Detoxification:	The process of allowing the body to metabolize drugs, excrete them, and become drug-free.
Drug dependence:	The state of being in need of further doses of a drug to maintain feelings of physical or psychological well-being.
EMCDDA:	The European Monitoring Centre for Drugs and Drug Addiction. Established in 1993 and based in Lisbon, it is the central source of comprehensive information on drugs and drug addiction in Europe.

Gateway drug:	A drug whose use is said to lead on to the use of other, often more dangerous, drugs.
Gravity pipe:	A device for smoking cannabis using gravity to draw cannabis smoke into the chamber of a pipe and then push it out through the pipe mouthpiece.
Hair screening:	A method of testing for substance use using hair samples.
Halfway houses:	A supportive residential establishment for those who have completed detoxification/rehabilitation, prior to them returning to independent living.
Herbal cannabis:	The dried and chopped leaves and flower heads of the cannabis plant, usually compressed into bales of varying sizes.
Hot knifing:	A method of smoking cannabis where a heated knife blade is applied to the drug to release smoke.
Hydroponics:	A method of growing plants involving nutrient-rich solutions as a growing medium, rather than soil.
Joint:	A hand-rolled cannabis cigarette.
Named patient basis:	A scheme which allows a doctor to prescribe an unlicensed drug to a particular 'named patient'.
NDARC:	The National Drug and Alcohol Research Centre. Established at the University of New South Wales in May 1986. It is funded by the Australian government as part of their national drug strategy.
Paranoia:	A disturbed thought process characterized by excessive anxiety or fear, often to the point of irrationality and delusion.
Potency:	A measure of the ability of a drug to produce the effect desired by the user. The higher the potency, the smaller the amount of drug required.
Psychosis:	A broad term used to describe severe mental disorders where people may lose sight of reality without realizing they are unwell.
Psychotherapy:	The treatment of psychological conditions without the use of medication. Includes such treatments as counselling and cognitive behavioural therapy.
Rehabilitation:	A blanket term for techniques including pharmaceutical and psychological therapies in the treatment of substance dependency.
Reward pathway:	A number of structures involved in the release of dopamine, including the nucleus accumbens and the ventral tegmental area, within the limbic system of the human brain, all connected by the medial forebrain bundle of axons.
Roach:	A small piece of card inserted in the mouth end of a hand-rolled cannabis cigarette.
Roach card:	Usually a colourful advertising card that is perforated to enable the user to divide it into 'roach'-sized pieces.
Rubbing:	A traditional method of producing cannabis resin in which the trichomes bearing the resin are rubbed from the plant and collected.
Saliva screening:	A method of testing for substance use using oral fluids.
Schizophrenia:	A serious mental disorder which can result in profound changes to a patient's personality, perception and behaviour.
Skunk or super-skunk:	A highly potent form of cannabis produced by selective cross breeding of the three main cannabis varieties, and then cloning for true growing seeds.

Terpenes:	Any of a number of combinations of hydrocarbons found in the essential oils of certain plants including cannabis, contributing to its characteristic smell.
Threshing and sieving:	A traditional method of producing cannabis resin, in which the dried plant material is passed through a series of sieves.
Toke can:	A crude smoking pipe made from a drinks can.
Tolerance:	The state arrived at with repeated use of a drug, where increasing doses are needed to achieve the desired effect.
Trichomes:	Small hair-like structures growing on the leaves and flower buds of the cannabis plant.
UN *World Drug Report*:	A comprehensive report published annually by the UN Office on Drugs and Crime.
Urine screening:	A method of testing for substance use using urine samples.
Vaporizer:	A device designed to raise the temperature of cannabis to its vaporization point, whilst staying below its ignition temperature.
Water extraction:	A traditional method of producing cannabis resin in which dried cannabis is shredded and then mixed with water. The heavier resin sinks, whilst the remaining plant material floats on the water.
Water pipe:	A device for smoking cannabis in which the smoke is drawn through water before reaching the smoker.
Withdrawal Syndrome:	A collection of symptoms, some or all of which may occur when the use of a particular drug is discontinued.

Appendix Two

Self-Help and Support to Quit
or Reduce Usage

The following websites offer advice on giving up or reducing cannabis use. The inclusion of any particular website should not be taken as implying that we are recommending them or the advice that they give. However, in our view, they are worth studying by anyone seeking help with cannabis use problems. All websites accessed on 22 August 2008.

UK

A website providing a free downloadable pdf document entitled *A Guide to Cutting Down and Stopping Cannabis Use.*
www.knowcannabis.org.uk/images/Kclargeguide.pdf

US

A website offering downloadable guides to quitting cannabis use.
www.cannabisaddicts.com/

Another website offering downloadable guides to quitting cannabis use.
https://stopsmokingcannabis.org/Home_Page.html

Australia

A website providing a free downloadable pdf document entitled *Getting Out of it: How to Cut Down or Quit Cannabis.*
www.edas.org.au/docs/cannabis.pdf

A website providing a free downloadable pdf document entitled *Making Changes: A Self-Help Package for People Thinking about Changing their Lifestyles.*
www.gsahs.nsw.gov.au/UserFiles/File/Microsoft%20Word%20-%20cannabis%20making%20changes.pdf

Rehabilitation, Detoxification and Treatment Services

The following websites offer information regarding available drug rehabilitation and detoxification services. The inclusion of any particular website should not be taken as implying that we are recommending them as the best source of such information. They simply provide a useful place to start one's search for such services in any particular locality. All websites accessed on 22 August 2008.

UK

Drug Rehab and Drug Addiction Services

Provides an information portal listing treatment organizations across the UK.
www.uk-rehab.com

US

Drug Rehabs

Provides information and treatment resources for individuals suffering all addictions. Referrals to treatment centres across the US are offered at no charge as a community service.
www.drug-rehabs.com

Canada

Alcohol and Drug Rehab Directory

Provides links to Canadian Drug and Alcohol Rehab Centres and Detox Centres, offering substance abuse treatment services throughout Canada.
www.alcohol-drug-rehab-directory.com/canada.htm

Australia

Australian Drug Information Network

Lists treatment organizations across Australia.
www.adin.com.au/content.asp?Document_ID=38

New Zealand

Addictions Treatment Directory

Lists treatment organizations across New Zealand.
www.adanz.org.nz/Services/Home

South Africa

12 Step Treatment Centres

Lists treatment organizations across South Africa.
www.12steptreatmentcentres.com/Display_Results.asp?Search=Basic&cboCountry=163

Useful Organizations

The following organizations may be of help to anyone seeking further information, help or support for a drug or substance problem. All websites accessed on 22 August 2008.

UK

DrugScope

Formed by the amalgamation of ISDD (Institute for the Study of Drug Dependence) and Scoda (Standing Conference on Drug Abuse). Provides expert information, training and resources.

40 Bermondsey Street
London SE1 3UD
Tel: 020 7940 7500
Fax: 020 7940 7521
Email: info@drugscope.org.uk
Website: www.drugscope.org.uk

Narcotics Anonymous

A non-profit fellowship of men and women for whom drugs have become a major problem.

UK Service Office
202 City Road
London EC1V 2PH
Tel: 020 7251 4007
Fax: 020 7251 4006
24/7 helpline: 0845 3733366
Email: ukso@ukna.org
Website: www.ukna.org

Frank/National Drugs Helpline

Provides information and access to help for all those concerned about drugs.

Free confidential 24-hour service to users, their families and friends.

Tel: 0800 77 66 00

Website: www.talktofrank.com

Website provides email services for those wishing to seek further information.

Parentline Plus

UK registered charity that offers support to anyone parenting a child.

520 Highgate Studios
53–79 Highgate Road
Kentish Town
London NW5 1TL
Free helpline: 0808 800 2222
Website: www.parentlineplus.org.uk

Release

24-hour advice, information and referral on legal and drug-related problems for users, their families and friends.

388 Old Street
London EC1V 8LT
Administration tel: 020 7729 5255
Helpline: 0845 4500 215
Website: www.release.org.uk

Northern Ireland Community Addiction Service HO

NICAS works at community level providing a service for people who are abusing alcohol and drugs and dealing with people who are concerned about alcohol and drugs.

40 Elmwood Avenue
Belfast BT9 6AZ
Tel: 028 9066 4434
Fax: 028 9066 4090
Website: www.communityni.org/index.cfm/section/finder/key/5275

Scottish Drugs Forum

The national, voluntary sector and membership-bascd drugs policy and information agency working in partnership to reduce drugs harm in Scotland.

91 Mitchell Street
Glasgow G1 3LN
Tel: 0141 221 1175
Fax: 0141 248 6414
Email: enquiries@sdf.org.uk
Website: www.sdf.org.uk

US

Drug Enforcement Administration

The national organization responsible for the enforcement of substance control laws in the US.

For mail directed to DEA headquarters
Mailstop: AES
2401 Jefferson Davis Highway
Alexandria, VA 22301
Website: www.usdoj.gov/dea/index.htm

National Institute on Drug Abuse

NIDA's mission is to lead the nation in bringing the power of science to bear on drug abuse and addiction.

6001 Executive Boulevard, Room 5213
Bethesda, MD 20892-9561 US
Tel: 301-443-1124 or 240-221-4007 en español
Email: information@nida.nih.gov
Website: www.nida.nih.gov/NIDAHome.html
To obtain downloadable information on cannabis, go to:
www.nida.nih.gov/MarijBroch/Marijintro.html

National Clearinghouse for Alcohol and Drug Information

Information and advice concerning substance abuse.
Website: http://ncadi.samhsa.gov

The website provides email services for those wishing to seek further information.

Canada

Canadian Centre on Substance Abuse/National Clearing House on Substance Abuse

Information and advice concerning substance abuse.

112 Kent Street
Suite 480
Ottawa KIP 5P2
Tel: 613 235 4048
Website: www.ccsa.ca

Australia

The Alcohol and other Drugs Council of Australia

Non-government organization representing the interests of the Australian alcohol and other drugs sector, providing a national voice for people working to reduce the harm caused by alcohol and other drugs

Postal address: PO Box 269, Woden, ACT 2606
Street address: 17 Napier Close, Deakin, ACT 2600
Tel: 02 6281 0686
Fax: 02 6281 0995
Email: adca@adca.org.au
Details of helplines at www.adca.org.au/content/view/31/56
National Cannabis Information and Helpline 1800 30 40 50

New Zealand

National Society on Alcohol and Drug Dependence (NSAD)

Provides advice and literature on drug matters.

PO Box 9183
Wellington
Tel: 04 385 1517
Website: www.nsad.org.nz

New Zealand Drug Foundation

Provides advice and literature on drug matters.

PO Box 3082
Wellington
Tel: 04 499 2920
Fax: 04 499 2925
Website: www.nzdf.org.nz

South Africa

SA Health Info

One-stop shop for reviewed, evidence-based health information focusing on southern Africa.

Prof. C. Parry
Medical Research Council
PO Box 19070
Tygerberg 7505
South Africa
Tel: +27 219380419
Email: charles.parry@mrc.ac.sa
Website: www.sahealthinfo.org/sahealthinfo.htm

Index